DOG TRAINING PROJECTS FOR YOUNG PEOPLE

BY
JOEL M. MCMAINS

PHOTOS BY
ANITA NICHOLS AND THE AUTHOR

HOWELL BOOK HOUSE
MACMILLAN • USA

OTHER HOWELL BOOKS
BY JOEL M. McMAINS

DOG LOGIC: COMPANION OBEDIENCE
Rapport-Based Training

ADVANCED OBEDIENCE:
Easier Than You Think

KENNELS AND KENNELING

Howell Book House
A Simon & Schuster Macmillan Company
1633 Broadway
New York, NY 10019

MACMILLAN is a registered trademark of Macmillan, Inc.

ISBN 0-87605-506-4

Library of Congress Cataloging-in-Publication Data

McMains, Joel M
        Dog training projects for young people / by Joel M. McMains; photos by Anita Nichols and the author.
                p.   cm.

        1. Dogs–Training–Juvenile literature.   [1. Dogs–Training.]
I. Nichols, Anita, ill.   II. Title.
SF431.M468   1995   95-24669
636.7'0887–dc20   CIP
                                                                                       AC

Manufactured in the United States of America

CONTENTS

FOR RON FLATH

caring friend, gifted teacher

Someday, after we have mastered the winds, the waves, the tides and the gravity, we shall harness for God the energies of love. Then, for the second time in the history of the world, man will have discovered fire.

PIERRE TEILHARD DE
CHARDIN

PREFACE

This is a book about children and dogs, teaching and training, giving and receiving. Based in part on material in *Dog Logic: Companion Obedience* and *Advanced Obedience: Easier Than You Think*, the manual includes training program start-ups, organization and record keeping. It offers training and competition approaches in obedience, conformation, showmanship and tracking. It also covers teaching techniques, grooming and problem solving. The book does not examine each and every practice and regulation found in every US state and county, however. Variations in how programs are conducted regionally will always exist, so to represent this text as comprehensive in that sense would be misleading. Obviously, that is not my intent.

I write from the viewpoint of a 4-H dog project leader, as that's where my background is strongest, having been involved with 4-H dog projects since 1982. That's not to imply that 4-H endorses this book. It can't. It has rules prohibiting official endorsement of commercial products. However, after reviewing the manuscript, Jon E. Irby, interim assistant deputy administrator at 4-H's national headquarters in Washington, DC, wrote in a letter to me:

> We are impressed with the great deal of excellent information you have included in your book in an easy-to-read style, and expect this manual would be very helpful to many youth interested in dog projects regardless of their organizational affiliation.

Given that happy, knowledgeable youngsters and happy, reliable dogs are a primary goal, this book should serve as a basis for any type of dog training project for children, regardless of organizational ties. The book is intended for teachers and parents as well as students. It operates from the premise that young readers have little if any formal knowledge about dogs or training them. Also, because knowledge of dogs and training varies among instructors, I presume only that teachers are familiar with the basics (including how to deal with aggressive dogs), enjoy working with groups of people of all ages and have abiding love for man's best friend.

Dog Training Projects for Young People is not represented to contain all the dog and training knowledge in the world. Obedience training and bonding are more than adequately covered, but not to the depth offered in *Dog Logic: Companion Obedience* and *Advanced Obedience: Easier Than You Think*. Conformation showing and showmanship are thoroughly presented, but not to the same degree as in *The Winning Edge: Show-Ring Secrets* by George Alston and Connie Vanacore. No, I haven't cut corners on the necessities. The book is not merely a primer; it includes information students, instructors and parents need to know. But to compile a comprehensive text about teaching, training and the human-canine relationship, and to also include grooming, care and general dog knowledge while also presenting material generally applicable to the programs of various organizations, would be to spawn an unwieldy tome that might tax a reader's endurance even more than this sentence does! In the words of Pascal, "Too much . . . education hinders the mind."

Though competition is available to young people, and training is somewhat geared for competition, it's not mandatory. If a student wants to compete with his or her dog, that's fine. But if a student prefers to avoid the ring, wishing instead only to learn about and enjoy his or her pet, that's fine, too. No child should be pushed into an area of discomfort. The relationship between child and dog is of such a special and enduring nature that mentions of ribbons and trophies in the same breath are inappropriate. Keep an open mind. Be flexible and receptive. A dog project can be a rewarding learning experience for everyone—not just for students or dogs, but for *everyone*. Children, instructors, parents and officials alike may be surprised at how much each can teach the other, and how much the dogs can teach all, provided they're allowed to.

ACKNOWLEDGMENTS

Thank you, good people, for your help in putting this one together: Ron Flath, Jim Robinson, Jo Sykes, Beverly Gorzalka, Cel Hope, Linnet McGoodwin, Gene Rohrbeck, Marilyn Mills, Sharon Michael and Rhea Regan. Special thanks are offered to Laurie Schwaubauer for patient assistance with the grooming and conformation chapters, Roger Davidson and Avril Roy-Smith for their eye-tiring proofreading, and Seymour Weiss, my editor at Howell Book House. I also thank every youngster I've ever had the pleasure of instructing, with gratitude for the lessons and memories they and their dogs have given me.

SECTION
I

PERSPECTIVES

1 FOCUS ON STUDENTS

FROM MYTH TO REALITY

Do you know what a myth is? It's something that might sound right, but really isn't true. Here's an example: A child can't train a dog as well as an adult can. That's a complete myth. It "sounds" right because grownups are bigger and stronger, so they can do some things more easily than children can. But training a dog is *not* necessarily among those actions.

The reality is this: Young people have many advantages over adults as dog trainers. The greatest is that kids naturally and uninhibitedly empathize with their pets. As understanding is the key to training any animal, kids possess innate talent!

Your dog's love for you and your warmth for your dog will lead you past many seeming barriers. Even if you only teach "Sit!" you should expect your pet to be police-dog reliable to the command. There's a good chance your companion can be that dependable, and that you can train your dog that well. So, if you ever hear anyone say that a youngster can't train a dog as well as an adult can, remember to tell yourself, "That's a myth."

"BUT, IT'S SO EASY FOR MY TEACHER"

Sure, professionals can make it look easy. They've developed a touch for their work. But the truth is the pro knows it *is* easy to deal with animals that for the most part are quite happy to be dealt with. The willingness of dogs to be led and to delight in human companionship makes up much of their attraction for us in the first place. If this weren't true, maxims like "man's best friend" wouldn't exist; dogs wouldn't occupy the special place in our hearts that they do.

HEAD START

This book is structured so you can train your dog with no additional help. Still, you're miles ahead of the game if you have someone to help you, a person you can ask questions and talk things over with. Someone who knows and can communicate with dogs and who can show you what you need to know can not only save you much time and effort, but can bring you and your pet closer together. If you find yourself in the company of such an individual who seems genuinely interested in helping you, count your blessings and listen up: You're being offered a tremendous gift.

GOOD THINGS COME IN THREES

Dog projects traditionally offer three types of training and competition: conformation, showmanship and obedience. Conformation pertains to the quality of the dogs, how closely each dog matches the definition (the written Standard) of its breed. Showmanship refers to how skillfully you handle your dog in conformation competition, your abilities in the ring. Obedience is how well your pet obeys you. If a dog has to be told "Sit!" several times, that's not obedience. Pooch may know what "Sit!" means, but he doesn't know he has to do it.

YOUR SPECIAL DOG, YOUR SPECIAL FRIEND

Don't ever let anyone tell you that real dog training means you stop caring for your companion; that you should now treat him mechanically, like some sort of object. That's not only foolish, it's another myth. Here's something I tell beginning students at their first class. Think about what follows because it can help you and your dog.

Let's think for a moment about your attitude. You know why you're here today, yes? To start learning about dogs and training. Sure. But how does your pet see it? Do you really think he knows what's going on? That he's here to be trained? Give me a break! More important, give your dog one. For all Pooch knows, today's get-together isn't much different from just another trip to the vet. We can't tell him what's going on; we'll have to show him.

Now, this is a dog you're dealing with, not a person. I know, that's obvious. But I also know that after a few lessons, students sometimes say that training a dog is like teaching a person. And I agree—some things seem the same. But it's unkind to think of a dog as a human or to treat him like one. A dog is always happiest treated fairly and kindly as a dog than as anything else.

So don't compare your pet to a person, or to someone else's dog. That's a trap, a very dangerous one. Appreciate your pal for what he is, not for what he isn't. Otherwise you ignore what he is, and that can set him up for a lifetime of disappointment. It can damage the dog's spirit and interfere with the bonding process. A dog trapped in a situation like that will always worry that you aren't satisfied with him. What he will never understand is why.

I want you to be careful about something else, too: getting too wrapped up in training for its own sake. A person can become so fascinated with how training is done and how it works that how *becomes more important than* who. *A trainer can begin to see Pooch as an object, a thing, instead of the caring, loyal friend and partner he truly is.*

Today you guys are very much in tune with your pets. You hear their inner voices, like they hear yours. Hang on to that—it's precious, a gift that's worth more than all the ribbons and trophies in the world.

SOMETHING SPECIAL

Of the many things I give my students to read, Ten Commandments seems to be their favorite. I hope you enjoy it, too.

TEN COMMANDMENTS[*]

My life is likely to last ten to fifteen years. Any separation from you will be painful for me. Remember that before you buy me.

Give me time to understand what you want of me.

Place your trust in me—it's crucial to my well-being.

Don't be angry at me for long, and don't lock me up as punishment. You have your work, your entertainment, and your friends. I have only you.

Talk to me sometimes. Even if I don't understand your words, I understand your voice when it's speaking to me.

Be aware that however you treat me I'll never forget it.

---

[*]From the computer program Canis; used with permission of Centron Software Technologies. Canis is excellent software for record keeping, resource information and all-around enjoyment. The program is available from Centron, 1500 N.W. 3rd St. Suite 101 Deerfield Beach, Florida, 33442 (305) 425-0557.

Remember before you hit me that I have teeth that could easily crush the bones of your hand but that I choose not to bite you.

Before you scold me for being uncooperative, obstinate or lazy, ask yourself if something might be bothering me. Perhaps I'm not getting the right food, or I've been out in the sun too long or my heart is getting old and weak.

Take care of me when I get old; you too will grow old.

Go with me on difficult journeys. Never say, "I can't bear to watch it," or, "Let it happen in my absence." Everything is easier for me if you are there. Remember, I love you.

REFLECTION

You see things and you say, "Why?" But I dream things that were never there and I say, "Why not?"

GEORGE BERNARD SHAW

CHAPTER 2
FOCUS ON PARENTS

This section appears in the chapter for parents because they often have the final say about who teaches their children. Though instructors are theoretically under the sole direction of the local arm of the organization for which they work, and regardless of whether parents formally evaluate instructors, if enough moms and dads disapprove of a teacher, that person's program days are numbered.

So parents, this one's aimed at you and I suggest you carve it in stone: When it comes to instructors, don't just settle for what you can get. Unlike veterinarians, trainers are not universally required to be licensed or certified. Yet, like a vet, a teacher can scar a dog—or a child—with long-lasting, harmful effects. A "wrong" instructor can be worse than no instructor at all.

Look for someone who can develop rapport with children, and who can teach. If neither qualification is met, keep looking. A person uncomfortable around children is of no more value to a dog-based project than is someone who can't communicate ideas. Once you find someone adept in both areas—and you will if you're determined and patient—*then* concern yourself with the individual's training knowledge and skills.

It might be nice if the services of a veteran trainer could be had, but that's not always possible. It's also not always the best course. The idea that any trainer would be a good teacher, especially of young people, just doesn't follow; some excellent trainers would make terrible instructors. Those having little patience with people are seldom comfortable in groups of more than two. Most recognize this in themselves and are wise enough to shun teaching. There's no disgrace in that. We all have our limitations and comfort zones, and a wise person respects and honors his or her gifts without pushing beyond individual abilities.

WHERE TO LOOK FOR INSTRUCTORS

Start with local dog clubs, especially those offering training classes. That may be a good starting point as you'll have opportunities to meet local dog people. And even if the group's trainer is neither right nor available for your group, you may meet someone who is.

Ask to observe a training session before soliciting anyone's help. If the sponsors are unreceptive to your request, that's a good reason to avoid them. If you're allowed to attend—it is hoped the group will encourage your request—keep an open mind. You may witness seemingly harsh discipline that in reality may be appropriate to the situation.

In judging an instructor's worth, consult the following list[*]:

Does your dog approve of the instructor?

What kind of rapport exists between the instructor and his/her own (demonstration) dog?

Does the instructor teach the dogs, or the owners?

Can the instructor instruct?

Does the instructor explain?

Is the instructor responsive, flexible?

Is the instructor tolerant?

Is the instructor knowledgeable?

Can the instructor handle a critical situation?

My belief is that a skillful instructor shares rather than controls, guides rather than orders. Such a person has no tolerance for canine abuse and inexhaustible patience with students. A "professional" instructor knows that the program, regardless of organizational affiliation, is for and belongs to the children.

ONCE YOU FIND A GOOD TEACHER

Let the person do the job. Sure, if you have ideas for the program, offer them. If you see something you think the instructor is missing, speak

---

[*]Taken from *Top Working Dogs: A Training Manual*, page 30, by Dietmar Schellenberg. This excellent book is available from D.C.B., 1164 Wall Road, Webster, NY, 14580.

up. But if you observe training or teaching techniques you don't understand, realize the obvious: You don't understand. That could be why you're not teaching the classes. It may be the instructor knows exactly what he or she is doing, and that your teaching and canine knowledge is insufficient to allow you to understand what you're seeing. If most of the children and their pets seem to like the person and if progress is being made, though you may not see why the teacher is doing a given thing in a given way, or isn't doing things the way you would, leave well enough alone. Much wisdom resides in the observation, "If it ain't broke, don't fix it."

In my 4-H classes I encouraged students and parents alike to "Ask if you don't understand," my thinking being that knowledgeable parents are better able to support their children's efforts. However, be aware the full statement I make is, "Kids, if you don't understand something, ask. Parents: Please do your asking *after* class."

Last, consider this: There is a thin line between a youngster being someone's child and being someone else's student. Just as we must honor boundaries in dealing with those outside our family, parents must let their children be an instructor's students.

AID AND COMFORT

Now, does all this mean parents, relatives and friends can't assist the program? Of course not. My attitude toward people who want to help is not just "Yes!" but "Thank God—Yes!" I won't detail here the many ways adults can be of service—the assistance needed is often dependent upon the training area's physical layout, the number of students and instructors involved and so forth. The kind of help generally needed takes many forms. Attendance should be taken, records must be maintained, the training site must be cleaned after each use, dogs' muddy paws may need toweling before entering a building, training equipment must be made, a few folks on the lookout for a dogfight's flash point can prevent trouble before it starts and crowds of people make for excellent conditioning for competition.

IMPOSSIBLE SITUATIONS

Can your child physically control his or her dog during a high-stress situation? If the answer is "No," or even "Probably not," don't put the youngster in the impossible position of trying to work with that particular animal.

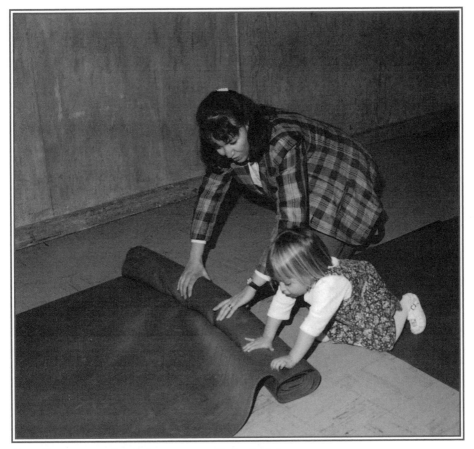

Virtually anyone can be of help to a community dog project.

First, it's potentially demoralizing for the child: If the youngster can't handle the dog, he or she will achieve only limited success while learning the feeling of frustration.

Second, it's unsafe for all concerned. Dogfights can start in a blink, and when a child is paired with a dog he or she can't control, the result can be at least one ripped-up kid. If you suspect Pooch is too much for your child to handle, or if the animal is aggressive toward other dogs, protect everybody by acquiring a dog more suited to the child's abilities or by keeping the youngster out of the program.

A physically safer situation, but one that can be equally damaging to a child's self-esteem (not to mention the dog's), is enrolling him or her with a virtually untrainable animal. No, you don't have to shop for

Given the size mismatch, this youngster might have a better chance at riding the Newfoundland than at leash control.

the next Lassie, but it's pointless to send a child to class with a thirteen-year-old dog that has never seen a leash or collar, or one that can't seem to remember where its food dish is from one day to the next.

If your family pet isn't right for a young people's dog training program, or if you're looking for a dog but must watch your budget, consider whether a dog of mixed parentage or a rescue dog might do. Companionship is where you find it, and no correlation exists between canine affection and purebred versus mixed-breed. Besides, a staggering number of such unwanted dogs are destroyed annually. The right dog might be waiting for you at the local shelter, where you'll also find homeless purebreds.

DON'T PUSH—ENCOURAGE

The child hadn't lost interest in dog training so much as other pursuits were pulling at her. She'd been in our local 4-H project for a number of years, had raised her dog from a puppy, had done well in the program and was ready to explore other worlds. It's called growth. Still, I overheard her dad threaten, "Either you stay in 4-H or we'll get rid of your dog!"

Raise your blood pressure some? It did mine. I asked Dad if he and I might have a word, we stepped away from the group and I told him that no child's pet should be used as an emotional battering ram. He told me to mind my own business, so I visited with Mom and she reportedly told Dad that if he got rid of the dog, she'd shed herself of him. The dog stayed!

It's an extreme case, sure, but it makes the point: Extortion is wrong. When perpetrated upon kids, it's nothing less than abuse.

Consider other verbal censure I've heard over the years:

"You can have a dog but only if you take him to 4-H."

"I guess that's a nice enough ribbon, but how come you let someone else win first place?"

"That dog's dumber than you are."

"You get straight A's in school or you can't keep your dog."

"Your dog is sure a funny-looking thing."

Absurd statements, aren't they? My experience suggests that 90 percent of the parents reading this book would never treat their children in such an obdurate or callous manner. So why is this section necessary? Unfortunately, it's needed for the children of the remaining 10 percent.

HOMEWORK

If your child asks questions at home about class, of course you should help where you can. Similarly, if you observe your youngster seems to have forgotten a lesson or is applying it improperly, have a word with him or her. However, keep in mind that training and caring for Pooch is the child's responsibility, not yours. Sure, you should feed the dog should your child be unable to. But if you hear "Lady won't sit! I quit!" or "I'd rather watch TV," don't do your youngster's homework.

REFLECTION

The way you activate the seeds of your creation is by making choices about the results you want to create. When you make a choice, you mobilize vast human energies and resources which otherwise go untapped. All too often people fail to focus their choices upon results and therefore their choices are ineffective. If you limit your choices only to what seems possible or reasonable, you disconnect yourself from what you truly want, and all that is left is a compromise.

ROBERT FRITZ

CHAPTER

3 FOCUS ON INSTRUCTORS

WELCOME TO DOG TRAINING 101!

That's how I open first-week meetings. The idea is to entice attention while putting students at ease. My intent is also to set the tone, because while the time has indeed come for some serious dog training, that doesn't imply that trainers of any age must leave their senses of humor and compassion at the door.

Perspective can be lost all too easily during this sort of work. That's a potential pitfall for which you should be continually alert and that you may need to stress to some students. Too often some people see what properly applied force can quickly and easily effect, but being new to the game, that's all they see. They can forget just who is at leash's end. A twofold obligation of instructing, then, is to educate the student and to protect the dog.

OBLIGATIONS

An instructor can profoundly influence not only student and dog, but their relationship as well. Though it's true a knowledgeable trainer may "know" a student's dog after a few minutes to a greater depth than the student ever will, keep in mind this knowing is usually the type that's of interest only to trainers: Breed and gender tendencies, temperament, instinct and drive levels, and so forth. No one can know that dog like the student does, in terms of affection, companionship and as a member of the family. Whether you or I see a given dog as having great potential or very little is immaterial and irrelevant; it's none of our business. The youngster cares a great deal for the animal and there's an end to it. It's a sin to come between them by any means, from judgmental pronouncements to the subtle, undercutting effects of raised eyebrows or disparaging, "What am I going to do with this kid?" sighs.

Realize, too, that youngsters can't always pick their dogs. Kids are often saddled with whatever dog is available, usually the family pooch that is seldom superstar material. This is because most parents, not being "dog people," don't realize that some canines are more trainable than others.

I mention these points because a question you'll be asked time and again is, "What do you think of my dog?" Answer: Find something positive to say about every dog. Am I suggesting you should lie? No. You won't have to. Just do a little looking and you'll find worth in any dog. A person who can't do that doesn't belong in dog-related activities, certainly not in the teaching department. A student who seeks your opinion about his or her pet is in truth seeking your approval. Sure, the love emanating from the dog's eyes toward the child should be all the answer anyone ever needs, but some children (and some adults) need a little propping up from time to time, for a host of reasons. Pooch may not be your idea of the "Right Dog"—he may not even come close—but to the youngster, that's a very special friend at leash's end, or at least one he or she wants to be special. Maybe all it will take to tip the scale permanently is your reassuring, "He's a heck of a nice dog; I think you're both very lucky."

LIKEWISE

A trap into which some instructors fall is demanding too much. A teacher can project such exacting standards that some students and dogs won't have a chance of measuring up. Especially prone are trainers experienced with adults but not children. The pupils and their charges may be doing quite well, but if the instructor fails to acknowledge their successes, or cheapens their triumphs by accenting the negative through continual nit-picking, kids may feel they or their dogs aren't performing up to snuff. Students can extend that to "There's something wrong with me and my dog," while in truth the problem is the teacher.

A subsection of *Dog Logic's* third chapter, "Pre-Training and Bonding," is "You're Always on Stage." It states that whenever an owner is near his dog, he's teaching the animal, regardless of intent. This is equally true in relating to students. They pick up signals (often without conscious realization) from your mannerisms, body language and choice of words. Of course, their inferences of your messages may be inaccurate. Though it may be tempting to rationalize, "The student misunderstood," the condition that may need to be addressed is, "I need to improve my communication skills."

This applies not just to specific lessons and techniques but to outlook as well. An ancient training adage is that the attitude a person sends down the leash comes back to him or her. That's also true in communicating with students. If your between-the-lines messages about relating with dogs include love, patience and respect, students may adopt these values in dealing with their pets. By the same token, radiating a philosophy of control, enforced subjugation and impersonal harshness validates such a stance as the "right way to do it." Remember, you're the *teacher*. You're in a position to affirm not just the correct way to hold a leash but the proper way to connect with our best friend. When you train a dog, you affect that one animal; when you teach classes you affect many, many dogs.

ATTRIBUTES

Some trainers are long on patience and forgiveness with dogs but short on tolerance of human frailties. One reason for this is that the dog only needs to know "What?" while the student may ask "Why?" The dog learns rapidly and accepts the obvious: The trainer is pack leader and is therefore in charge. The student, though he or she may be able to intellectualize training concepts quickly, takes longer to become proficient with the art's manual aspects.

When training a dog, the relationship can (and should) be expressed freely and openly. There are few rules to hamper or inhibit the development of understanding; expansion of rapport is limited only by the participant's ability to share it. Trainer and dog communicate empathetically at an extrasensory level, a feeling level, the oldest and deepest form of exchange. Posturing, game playing and "observing the amenities" aren't required. Trainer and dog can be themselves, together.

When a human student joins the situation, convention's need for protocol and formality can cause barriers to spring up—custom dictates that human social interaction be initiated at arm's length. In addition to age, gender, societal, background and expectation differences, boundaries—largely absent in the human-canine relationship—can get in the way. And in the classroom, communication can be inhibited even further because the setting superimposes an additional set of rules, regulations and role-sponsored restrictions.

Too, teaching a student requires considerably more effort than does training a dog. When a pooch doesn't respond to a command, the trainer consults a brief Yes-No checklist before deciding what action, if any, to take:

"Does the dog know the command?"

"Was he able to hear it?"

"Did I do something unusual when I gave the command that could have confused the animal?"

"Is there a distraction nearby for which the dog has not been conditioned?"

"Is command refusal characteristic of this dog?"

"Has the animal been having trouble with this command?"

"If I decide to correct the dog, what style should I use and with what degree of pressure?"

Though it's true a trainer mentally processes this before giving a command, programming his or her reaction to parallel the dog's response, the point remains that when teaching, a person is added to the equation and the variables become seemingly endless. The checklist is not only longer, its format becomes Yes-No-Maybe-Sometimes. Dogs perceive situations in black-and-white terms, but gray areas abound in human relationships and understanding. Thus, instructors are potentially faced with an endless stream of "What if?" "How come?" "Should I?" and so on.

Additional factors a teacher must weigh are the topic currently under discussion, the student's training and dog knowledge (or lack thereof), the student's personality, predisposition and abilities, the bonding level between person and dog, the student's feelings for the animal, his or her goals—the list goes on, and each element must be evaluated before proceeding.

Further, consider a point you'll encounter in chapter 7, "Obedience Training Guidelines": "Accept your pet's best attempts for what they are: his present best. He'll do better with time and encouragement. Fine-tune as you go along." The same principle applies to your manner of relating to students. People of any age generally do their best, especially in social settings. Sometimes their best may not seem very good, but that doesn't alter the fact that *it is their present best,* or that it may get better in time. If students err they simply need more of your help, which, I hope, is why you're both there.

JUST DO YOUR BEST, TOO

A healthy approach to teaching includes the realization that no instructor can reach every student. To deny this is to court disappointment. Better a teacher *try* to reach each student but without the unrealistic expectation of achieving the goal. Sound dogs are driven to learn, to see the consequences of their behaviors and choose a rewarding path. People can't always do this. Those who have made up their mind to resist an instructor will do so. Though such encounters are mercifully few, they do occur, and to maintain perspective you have to accept the fact. I'm not saying you have to like it; I'm saying you have to learn to live with it. To do otherwise is to premeditate frustration.

DECISION TIME

Though it's understandably a given that every dog project should have but one here's-where-the-buck-stops leader, which in this case is you, that doesn't imply that any leader should take a dictatorial stance. Leaders should lead, yes, but they should not compel a forced march. Our primary function is one of service. Assistants, parents, students and other concerned folk should not only be heard, they should be encouraged to speak up. Often they see things you and I might miss, just because we're too close to the action.

A related notion concerns the fact that some folks try to peddle rather than donate their efforts to community dog programs. My thought is the satisfaction derived from giving something back is worth far more than a few dollars.

IN CLOSING

Please read chapters 1 and 2, "Focus on Students" and "Focus on Parents." I talked about you in both of them. I wish you well.

REFLECTION

Be wiser than other people, if you
can, but do not tell them so.

LORD CHESTERFIELD

SECTION
II

GENERAL

4 PROJECT START-UP

Program creation requires children, their dogs, at least one instructor and project approval by the organization with which your group is affiliated. Additionally, the project should also include parental support, a place to meet, equipment and other miscellaneous items.

WHEN, WHERE AND HOW OFTEN?

Classes should meet weekly at the same time and place. More than one meeting a week is too much—many students will be involved in other activities—and holding classes less often, or frequently changing the meeting site or time, can disrupt continuity and dampen interest.

I've held classes at city parks, county storage buildings, horse barns, school gymnasiums and my own training yards. A school gym or similar building is best as it shuts out the elements and can be closed to outsiders. Class can be held after dark or in bad weather, and you don't have to be concerned that someone not associated with the program will wander into the area, get bitten or otherwise injured and take you to court.

The problem in using a school building can be securing permission from the powers that be. More than one school administrator has informed me: "Yes, your project's students are children and schools profess to serve children; and yes, a purpose of a community dog program is to educate children; and yes, the building would otherwise stand empty and unused; but no, the facility cannot be used for a non-school function."

Rather than reach for the aspirin, offer to stage an annual dog demonstration for the school, and promise to leave the facility immaculate after each meeting (and make sure the promise is kept). Look around and see if you have any school board friends who might intercede. Also, ask your organizational officials for help—they may be well connected with the local power structure.

HEAR YE! HEAR YE!

Ask your local organizational office to announce the first meeting a few weeks before the fact via its periodic bulletins sent to registered families. In addition to stating the place, date and time, require that parents attend at least the first session, and that each dog arrive on a secure six-foot leash and chain choke collar. Each animal's vaccination records should be brought to the first session (so you can verify all shots are current), and it should be stated that any dog not vaccinated against rabies, distemper and parvovirus (expand the list as you wish) will not be enrolled. Finally, give the minimum age for students that will be accepted into the class.

HOW TO START

Some classes require new students to begin with first-year obedience. The exception is children whose dogs already have sufficient training and socialization that they are under control. Further, we let first-year students compete in conformation and/or showmanship only with instructor approval, to protect children from taking on too much too soon.

CLASS SIZE

Class size is best kept to twelve students per instructor. This is not to say a class should be split into two sections should a thirteenth youngster

Our program requires two students a week to "volunteer" to sweep the practice site after class is over.

enroll. It is to say classes beyond a dozen or so become sufficiently unwieldy that personalized help can't be given.

Too, consider safety. A dozen untrained dogs per teacher can be risky enough; anything in excess of that number can be disastrous.

PAPERWORK

Have each parent sign a waiver absolving you of any and all liability related to project activities. Without such a release in your possession, you could be open for legal actions in the event of dog bites, theft of property, injury and other mishaps.

Don't settle for a student's signature on your form—minors cannot legally execute a binding contract. Also, obtain signed releases annually for *all* students, including those who have been in the program for several years. This ensures you always have current documents, which the courts like to see. Last, make sure to get a waiver not only for each student but for each dog. If a youngster is working with more than one animal, having a release for only one of the dogs could cause a legal nightmare should the other animal cause a serious problem.

Not incidentally, you should secure a waiver from any assistants, helpers and visitors. A sample enrollment form and waiver follows, as does a dog ID sheet, which is required by many organizations.* We use May 1 of the current year as the cutoff date. Of course, you should use whatever date meets your organization's guidelines.

JUST BEFORE THE FIRST CLASS

Before the first student's arrival, affix enrollment forms, waivers and dog ID sheets and pens to several clipboards. Avoid using tables as a sign-up area. Doing so brings dogs into close proximity with each other, and given that few untrained dogs will behave near new animals, the result can be a dogfight. Handing each arrival a clipboard allows him or her to complete your paperwork while moving a safe distance away. It also shortens enrollment time because clipboards can be circulated so no one has to wait for a spot to open at a sign-up location.

Inspect the training site for debris and foreign objects that could be injurious or distracting. If you're using an outdoor area, make certain no dog droppings are present that might stimulate class dogs to contribute.

---

*You are welcome to adapt all handout materials in this book provided you credit the source in writing: the book, author and publisher.

Finally, spend a few minutes alone. Relax. Center yourself. Meditate, if that's your style. A phrase from my youth is, "Get your head together." Teaching can be draining; make sure your tank is full before setting out. Release anxiety, put daily concerns on hold, clear your mind.

FIRST MEETING: NO TRAINING

That subtitle contains this section's message: No formal training should occur during the initial meeting. To train at a first session is generally to overwhelm the participants and can even make some nervous about returning. Keep it light during this first get-together. Let the children and their pets explore and get comfortable with the training site; use the time to get a reading on the students and their dogs. Welcome everyone to the program, get your waivers signed, outline the house rules (more about those in a moment) and see that proper leashes and collars are in use.

GIVE YOUR DOG A FEW DAYS OFF

Leave your dog at home for at least the first few sessions. Not only do you want your hands free during these initial meetings, bringing your pet to opening classes can be a study in boredom for the dog and can distract you and your pupils from the business at hand. Students appreciate a trained animal far more after a few weeks of working with their own charges.

Too, prematurely bringing in a trained dog can inhibit students. Contrary to your best intentions at class motivation, running your companion through its routines can make some people feel they'll never be able to train a dog to the degree you have, which, of course, remains to be seen.

HERE COMES EVERYBODY!

Once people begin arriving, make life easier for all concerned by observing that each dog is on a secure leash before alighting from its vehicle. It's wise to have a few extra leads and collars available for loan, if not for sale. Have everyone walk their animals well away from the working area before entry, to prevent fouling the training site.

As each enrollment form is completed, advise the student to walk the dog around the location, allowing the animals to sniff and explore the area but not each other. If trees are part of the setting, encourage everyone to keep their pets away from them lest the verticality principle come into play. Remind all participants that no dog is to contact another. Occasionally someone may ask, "If the dogs can't sniff each other, how will they ever become friends?" While the unspoken answer is that obedience training is the goal, not dog-to-dog friendship, explain you have three reasons for prohibiting sniffing.

First, it can transmit disease. Second, a training goal is teaching dogs to respond to their owners, not to other dogs. Allowing the animals to contact each other at the expense of tuning us out would subvert that message. Last, like people, bad chemistry can exist between dogs. All it takes is one "wrong" contact and a fight can result.

Of course, should a fracas occur you'll likely be the one to break it up. That would not only put you at risk but would cast a negative aura over the new class.

NOW IS THE HOUR

Wait a few minutes past the announced starting time before opening the meeting. It's disruptive for latecomers to arrive after you've begun, especially during the first session. Station yourself so everyone can hear you, and position students with a safe dog-to-dog distance. If an animal is unruly, either move that team farther away or take the leash and settle the offending canine to the extent you can proceed without further interruption, keeping the dog with you for the next few minutes if need be.

Affect a loose, relaxed, informal manner. An old training maxim is that a handler sends his or her own emotional state right down the leash and the dog reflects it. It's equally true that an instructor who mani-fests a rigid, overbearing, top-sergeant demeanor projects nervousness to students; they, in turn, transmit the attitude to their pets. Yes, some earnest training is going to occur during the next few weeks, but that doesn't mean an instructor must take him- or herself unreasonably seriously.

ATTENDANCE RECORDS

After verifying you have a current waiver for each student, make a list of the youngsters and keep track of attendance. See if a parent or two will help you with such paperwork. It allows them to participate and frees you for other tasks.

HOUSE RULES

After giving each student a copy of your rules and regulations, go over the list with them point by point. Then announce training will officially begin at the next session, that the purpose of today's meeting is to give everyone a chance to get used to the site. Ask if there are any questions, thank everyone for coming and close the meeting.

REFLECTION

No symphony orchestra ever played music like a two-year-old girl laughing with a puppy.

BERN WILLIAMS

[NAME OF COMMUNITY] DOG TRAINING PROJECT

ENROLLMENT

Please Print:

_____   _____   _____
(Student's Name & Age)   (Dog's Call Name)   (Age)

_____   _____   _____
(Address)   (Breed)   (Sex)

_____   _____
(City, State, Zip)   (Telephone)

Latest Vaccination Dates: _____ _____ _____
                          (Rabies)   (Distemper) (Parvo)

Have you trained a dog before? _____ Is dog registered? ____

Were you in a dog program last year? ____

What obedience level will you be in this year? (Circle one below)

> 1st-Year
>
> On-Leash
>
> Novice
>
> Grad. Novice
>
> Open
>
> Utility

What showmanship level will you be in this year?

> Junior
>
> Senior

[NAME OF COMMUNITY] DOG TRAINING PROJECT

WAIVER

I understand that attendance of a dog training class is not without risk to myself, to members of my family or guests who may attend, or to my dog(s), because some of the dogs to which I will be exposed may be difficult to control, and may be the cause of injury, even when handled with the greatest degree and amount of care.

I agree to hold the instructor(s) harmless for any claims for any loss or injury which may be alleged to have been caused directly or indirectly to any person or thing by the act of my dog while in or upon the training area, or near the entrance thereto, and I personally assume all responsibility and liability for any such claim; I further agree to hold the aforementioned party(s) harmless for any claim for damage or injury to my dog, whether such loss, theft, disappearance, damage, or injury be caused or be alleged to be caused by the negligence of the party aforementioned, or by the negligence of any other person, or any other cause or causes.

_____   _____

(Signature of Parent or Guardian)   (Date)

[NAME OF COMMUNITY] DOG TRAINING PROJECT

DOG I.D.

(Due May 1 of current year—no exceptions)

_____   _____
(Handler's Name)   (Dog's Call Name)

_____
(Dog's Registered Name)

_____
(Address)   (City, State, Zip)

_____
(Color & Description of Dog)

_____   _____
(Club Name)   (Date of Last Rabies Shot)

_____   _____
(Member's Home Phone)   (Date of Last Distemper/Hepatitis/
                                                         Leptospirosis/Parainfluenza/Parvo Shots)

_____   _____
(Member's Birthdate)   (Member's Social Security Number)

When was dog acquired for the Dog Project? _____
                                                                    Month/Day/Year

When was dog in your possession for the Dog Project? _____
                                                                         Month/Day/Year

_____ _____ _____
(Breed or Type)   (Variety)   (Sex)

Dog's Birthdate ____Place of Birth: USA ____Other _____

AKC Registration No. _____ AKC Litter No. _____

ILP Number _____

Other Purebred Registration No. and Breed _____

[NAME OF COMMUNITY] DOG TRAINING PROJECT

DOG I.D.

_____

Owner(s) Name

_____

Address

_____

City/State/Zip

    I certify that this dog is a project for the current year and is owned by myself or a member of my immediate family as required by [name of organization] policy. The owner must be an immediate family member—mother, father, brother, sister, or the member him/herself with the exception of co-owned dogs. I understand and will comply with the rules regarding valid proof-of-shots records before all sanctioned dog shows. Ownership may not be changed/added to/altered after May 1 of the current year.

_____

Signature of Member   Signature of Parent/Guardian

_____

Signature of Instructor

_____

Date Filed in Community Office   Signature of Agent

[NAME OF COMMUNITY] DOG TRAINING PROJECT

WELCOME TO DOG TRAINING 101!

Class will meet every [day] at [time] at [location] for about an hour. If a class has to be canceled you will be phoned before the scheduled time. During bad weather, if you haven't received a call saying class is canceled, *class is on.*

If you have to miss a class, don't give up. We'll help you catch up at the next session.

Wear comfortable tennis shoes to practice sessions, so you'll have better footing and won't risk hurting your dog's feet with heavy shoes or boots if you accidentally step on a foot.

Never bring a sick dog (or a female in season) to class, especially one with a bad cough. Leave Pooch home, but unless his condition requires you stay there with him, bring yourself, to keep up with what's going on.

When you arrive for class be sure your dog is on leash *before* it gets out of your vehicle. Remember: No dog is to touch or sniff another. We don't want a dogfight.

Walk your pet at home so it doesn't foul the training area. If your dog has an accident at class, it's *your* job to clean it up immediately and completely.

Anyone who abuses (kicks, beats, torments, screams at) a dog will be dismissed from the program.

Aggressive dogs are not allowed in the program.

Friends and family members are welcome to attend and observe the classes, provided they will remain quietly in one place and not be distractive.

We hope you'll enjoy these classes and that you'll tell your friends about them. Call one of the instructors if you need any help during the week. The evening hours are the best time to call. The phone numbers are [names and tele-phone numbers].

5 STUDENT RECORD KEEPING

Is student record keeping a necessary evil or a useful tool? In part the answer lies in your state and county requirements. Some organizations allow abolition of student record keeping. That's one extreme. Another is decreeing that students maintain such involved record books as to be projects unto themselves, leading one to wonder how the child finds time for the dog.

Keeping realistic project records offers many benefits. One is the scrapbook effect: providing students with memorabilia of their childhood. Too, it centralizes information that can help resolve issues, such as when a dog was vaccinated for what and by whom. A disadvantage to mandatory detailed records is the excessive time burden it imposes on students. This is especially true for the younger ones, many of whom are only beginning to master the written word.

My thought is: Record keeping is okay until it starts to interfere with the project itself, or when it becomes so demanding as to be drudgery. Then we have the tail wagging the dog. If record maintenance takes more than fifteen minutes weekly, something's wrong. Record keeping should serve the student, not the other way around.

One cause of overblown records is the fact that dog projects sometimes evolve as spin-offs from livestock programs. When a question arises about a fledgling dog project, a common response can be, "Well, what do we do in the cattle (or hog or sheep) program?" The thinking is that dogs, being animals, should be handled in a fashion similar to livestock management. Obvious disparities—have you ever heard of house-training a cow?—often go unnoticed. When managing cattle, hogs and the like, records of income and expense, for instance, are vital; but similar records for a dog project are not only superfluous, but such forms as "Inventory of Dogs and Equipment" subtly imply dogs are things.

Basic information can be recorded on ruled paper kept in a three-ring notebook or folder. There should be one notebook for each dog the student owns, not one notebook per year. As the relationship between dog and child is ongoing, so the records should be continual. Following are forms I prefer. Blank pages should be provided for photographs, awards and similar materials. Class handouts should also be kept in the notebook.

Students shouldn't have to keep track of routine expenses—food, vet care, basic equipment, leashes and collars. Such costs are attendant to proper care of any dog. Further, such information is confidential and, as one parent said, "is nobody's business."

Concepts such as having First-Year students list goals are all very well, but such ideas work better on paper than in the real world. One study I've read points out that 30 percent of all people entering college do so without declaring a major. Moreover, the average college student changes his or her major *at least* twice. I look at figures like those and wonder how a child is supposed to be able to project goals in a field of study he or she knows nothing about. It's unrealistic.

Finally, students shouldn't have to maintain a daily training log of what was done, when and for how long. Lessons taught should be checked off, and unusual training occurrences should be recorded, but to require an exhaustive itemization is to inhibit interest and enjoyment. Daily information may be recorded in the notebook, of course, but doing so should not be mandatory. Better the child should spend that time with the dog.

Besides, setting goals can limit perspective and desire. A student can become so tuned in to a given objective that he or she sees nothing else, no other directions, no other possibilities. Similarly, an individual having reached a goal can think, "I made it—now I can coast awhile." It's all very well to have a roadmap to point the way, but one mustn't be so rigid as to tune out the scenery, or to think there may be no other destinations.

REFLECTION

Much that passes for education is
not education at all but ritual.

DAVID P. GARDNER

[NAME OF COMMUNITY] DOG TRAINING PROJECT

PROJECT RECORDS

Student:_____ Age:_____Date Started: _____

Phone:_____ County:_____State: _____

Dog's Call Name:_____ Breed:_____Gender: _____

Tattoo Code:_____ AKC Registered Name:_____

AKC Registration Number:_____ Date of Birth: _____

Sire:_____ Sire's AKC Number: _____

Dam:_____ Dam's AKC Number: _____

Breeder: _____

Address: _____

Phone:_____ City, State:_____

Date Bought:_____

Vaccination Dates:

Rabies	Distemper	Parvo	Other
_____	_____	_____	_____
_____	_____	_____	_____
_____	_____	_____	_____
_____	_____	_____	_____
_____	_____	_____	_____
_____	_____	_____	_____
_____	_____	_____	_____

[NAME OF COMMUNITY] DOG TRAINING PROJECT

HEALTH HISTORY

Record dates/details about illnesses, worming and health care.

_____

_____

_____

_____

_____

_____

_____

_____

_____

_____

_____

_____

_____

_____

_____

_____

_____

_____

_____

_____

[NAME OF COMMUNITY] DOG TRAINING PROJECT

TRAINING NOTES

Check off exercises and levels completed. Record special situations, as well as training in addition to the exercises listed, in the area provided.

☐ **First-Year/On-Leash:**

☐ Heeling and Automatic Sit

☐ Sit-Stay

☐ Down-Stay

☐ Stand-Stay

☐ Over Jump at Heel

☐ Recall

☐ Finish

☐ **Novice:**

☐ Heel Off-Leash

☐ Sit-Stay

☐ Down-Stay

☐ Recall

☐ Finish

☐ **Graduate Novice:**

☐ Recall over High Jump

☐ Drop on Recall

☐ Sit-Stay (Out of Sight)

☐ Down-Stay (Out of Sight)

☐ **Open:**

☐ Retrieve on Flat Ground

☐ Retrieve over High Jump

☐ Broad Jump

☐ **Utility:**

☐ Scent Retrieve

☐ Directed Retrieve

☐ Stand from Motion

☐ Recall to Heel

☐ Send Out and Directed Jumping

☐ Hand Signals:

☐ Heeling

☐ Stay

☐ Down

☐ Sit

☐ Recall

☐ Finish

SECTION III

BEFORE OBEDIENCE TRAINING

CHAPTER 6

MAN'S BEST FRIEND AND YOU

As stated in the preface, this book is based upon the premise that young readers have little if any formal knowledge about dogs or training. This chapter examines exactly what a dog is, how dogs learn, what motivates them and how rapport and trainer attitude can shape the human-canine relationship.

WHAT IS A TRAINED DOG?

What does the term *trained dog* mean to you? I picture an animal that is reliable in all likely situations; its responses are predictable over a wide range of circumstances. Dogs that assist handicapped people, police or military dogs, herding dogs, circus dogs and some competition dogs belong in this category.

Notice, though, the term is not *well*-trained dog. *Well* would be a wasted word; it adds nothing because a dog is either reliable (trained) or he isn't (untrained). Dogs don't understand ideas like *maybe, almost* and *sort of.* A dog's way of looking at things is clear-cut, absolute: Do or do not, approach or avoid, yes or no, obey or ignore. That's why many professional trainers agree that half-trained is untrained.

So, does a trained dog never goof? Sure he does. Everyone makes a mistake now and then, dogs included. But in many ways a trained dog comes closer to working perfection than you or I, and his off days are fewer and further apart.

THE PACK CONCEPT

*Canis familiaris** is a semidomesticated pack animal; he's moderately tame and prefers to live with others instead of alone. His nature is to

*If you're ever asked the scientific name of the family dog, you'll be able to answer correctly.

submit to those he thinks are dominant, more powerful in mind and body than him. In turn, he tries to dominate those he thinks will submit. The dog doesn't choose this attitude; nature chooses it for him—he's driven toward his. He operates to ensure his survival through pack preservation. The way a dog sees things is: If his pack is threatened, he's threatened. A dog believes that without his pack, his own survival is at risk.

Each pack has a leader. Known as *alpha*, this animal's will is law. To become your dog's *pack leader* you must show him that you're dominant. You must demonstrate that Pooch need not apply for the *alpha* position—that job's been taken by you.

In other words, what you and I call a family your dog considers a pack. If you permit him to run you, he will. If you convince the dog you're dominant, he will accept your leadership. It's that simple. To accomplish anything worthwhile, instruction must match *the dog's* vision of reality—he's the one being taught.

Don't think a dog can be brought to our level. That can't happen. A dog will always be a dog, and no training method can change him, into some fuzzy kind of human being. We're trying to relate with a being that has neither the ability for speech nor a built-in understanding of any human language. A dog can learn to connect certain sounds (commands, praise, etc.) with actions on his part, but he can never comprehend the subtle meanings of words as you and I can. Tone of voice and body language are much more suitable to a dog's understanding.

RAPPORT

Rapport is both the means and the end, the seed and the flower. A dog may earn many ribbons, but if it has little or no affection for his owner, such honors mean little. Rapport is a mind-set, or a heart-set, as it were. It's an attitude, a way of feeling, a togetherness.

Equipment, like collars and leashes, is necessary to the training/bonding process. But depending on mechanical devices and seeing them as ends in themselves is limiting; reliance on gadgets can block development of friendship and bonding. Your attraction to your dog, properly communicated, will become the basis for its attraction to you. This attraction, in turn, becomes the basis of your pet's obedience, his reliability.

The concept of rapport-based training doesn't mean a dog should be begged to obey. The truth is each animal must be spoken to according to individual personality. With gentle dogs, very little training force is needed. With supertough animals, a sterner approach is appropriate. That's part of what is meant by working with each dog at his own level of understanding.

TRAINER'S ASSETS

Three traits of successful trainers are sincerity, a sense of humor and open-mindedness. Together they mold attitude.

Applied to dog training, "sincerity" means "be yourself." Don't play-act for your dog.

A sense of humor maintains perspective. Without the ability to laugh, especially at ourselves, capacities for forgiveness and learning are severely handicapped. Stern, inflexible types can place emotional barriers between themselves and their pets without being aware of having done so. Such folks can't distinguish between disobedience and simple nervous hesitancy.

The third element, open-mindedness, supports the other two. Trainers can't afford to lose a "Well, I'll be!" attitude when effective new approaches and methods come along. No trainer has all the answers, and when new and useful ideas are offered, they should be seen for the gifts they are.

IT'S A TWO-WAY STREET

The notion that only trainers may teach and only dogs may learn is not only faulty but dangerously limited thinking. Dog training is creating communication between two species, human and canine. You're reading this book to learn how. An irony is that your dog already knows how. He was born with an instinct to respect and obey the wishes of the pack leader.

There's no magic in training. It's far more art than science, as no system is "the only true way" (though some folks claim theirs to be). Methods can be described precisely but applying any method is an art. What you need to develop are communication skills so Pooch can understand you. In a phrase, you need to learn to "think dog." This book can teach you how, and if you listen to your pet, so can he.

REFLECTION

I am called a dog because I fawn
on those who give me anything, I
yelp at those who refuse, and I set
my teeth in rascals.

DIOGENES

7

OBEDIENCE TRAINING GUIDELINES

This chapter contains guidance for relating with man's best buddy. Other principles and techniques accompany lessons presented in other chapters.

OBEDIENCE TRAINING DEFINED

Obedience training is a process, not an event or a thing. It allows a person to control a dog by developing a basis for effective communication. It regulates Pooch's behavior by making him responsible for it. Obedience training also strengthens bonding by drawing the animal closer to the owner; it says to a dog, "You and I are together. Because I'm dominant. I lead." As suggested in the previous chapter, a sound dog recognizes this sentiment for what it is and the response is positive. That's a natural pack trait (and a main endearment) of all dogs.

OBEDIENCE TRAINING'S OBJECTIVE

Obedience training teaches several forms of work: sit, lie down, stay, come, heel, and so forth. In so doing it satisfies a dog's need for pack responsibility and identity. While the exercises have value in providing control, their greater purpose is making your pet responsive to you; to tune his ear to the sound of your voice, telling him you desire contact, you have things to teach, you two are a team.

SOME THINGS NEVER CHANGE

In 1925, Max Von Stephanitz, the "father" of the German Shepherd Dog, wrote: "Whoever can find the answer to the question, 'How shall I say this to my dog?' has won the game and can develop from his animal whatever he likes."*

Those timeless words are the essence of training, the "why" of it. Trainers sometimes blow right past the fact that there are reasons why training techniques do or do not work. A method is effective not because someone says it is; it's effective when and because a dog "says" it is. A dog "says" training is effective when the method produces a confident, reliable, happy worker. It's all very well to memorize a well-known trainer's system, but if a person doesn't understand how and why techniques work (or don't), he or she is training in the dark.

THE THREE STAGES OF TRAINING

Training occurs in three stages. First is *teaching*, passing along new material, new lessons. Second is *integration*, bringing separate exercises together; making one thing—obedience—out of the various commands being taught. The third phase, *conditioning*, is practicing under increasing distractions and in unfamiliar settings those things a dog has learned. All these elements taken together make up *training*.

Ultimately, training leads to *performance*, which is using conditioned learning in real-world situations. This phase is called *working*, but many trainers (myself included) think of *working* as also being the same as any of training's three elements.

TRAINING SESSIONS

WHEN AND NOT WHEN

Training is most effective when you have plenty of time and are not otherwise preoccupied. It's *not* when you or your pet is tired or ill, or when you are pressed for time. Negative feelings could go down the leash and could make your dog feel you're unhappy with him. That can produce nervousness in a relationship that should be worry-free.

NO SHADES, PLEASE

Leave your dark glasses in the house. Contact is a vital training concept and eye contact tops the list. A dog that can't see your eyes will eventu-

*Max von Stephanitz, *The German Shepherd Dog in Word and Picture*, Hoflin Publishing, Arvada, Colorado, 1982, page 564.

ally quit trying to. He learns not to look your way, which is exactly the opposite of the behavior you are trying to build.

ONLY YOU FOR NOW

For at least the first few weeks, Pooch should have only one trainer: you. A dog can have enough learning difficulties without the added confusion of one teacher's voice being different from another's. To a dog, a word spoken in a deep voice can sound different from the same word spoken in a high voice.

BEFORE A TRAINING PERIOD

Don't exercise or work your pet sooner than an hour after feeding. Doing so can not only cause cramping, it can lessen performance—a hungry dog works better. Also, provide time for Pooch to relieve himself before work or play.

Plan each practice, anticipating your pal's likely reactions to the day's lessons and determining how you'll respond. Planning and effective training go together.

NO INITIAL DISTRACTIONS

Teach in a distraction-free area. The notion that a dog is best taught near stressful surroundings is false. Distraction work (conditioning) should be delayed until the integration phase has been underway for several weeks.

CONSTANT TRAINING LOCATION

Confine the first weeks of training to one or two locations. Your dog will come to see the areas as special: They're not only a place for learning, but for correct behavior, too. The areas themselves act as reminders. Once Pooch is doing well with several commands, occasionally move practice sessions to more distractive locations.

YOUR PACK

Family members may attend practices but they should not speak your pet's name or make eye contact with it. Otherwise, Pooch can become confused and could learn to distrust other members of the family—his pack.

IT'S CALLED COMMITMENT

Be consistent in your training schedule. That's not to say, "Train daily at 5:17 PM," but train at least five days weekly. Pooch doesn't need an

Training is important but so is playtime. With just a Frisbee or a tennis ball, your dog not only gets good exercise, but the shared fun of playing with you, too.

occasional day off. You may, but your dog doesn't. He should look forward to the sessions.

HOW LONG?

Work your pet in fifteen- to twenty-minute periods. Twice daily is best (though not always possible), with several hours between sessions. And as you train for twenty minutes a day, play with your companion for twenty minutes a day.

CLASS VERSUS RECESS

Keep playtime separate from work periods for now. Your dog should wear the training collar during both activities*—to build good feelings toward him through the fun of play sessions—but do not give commands during play. Doing so too soon can lower enthusiasm.

END HIGH

End each training period on a positive note, with your dog doing an exercise correctly. Never quit in failure. That can lead your pet to carry a bad feeling into the next practice. If Pooch is having "one of those days," command something he knows well (like "Sit!"), and end the session with praise so he finishes with a success. Also, don't use commands when leaving the training area; should your pal goof and be disciplined, the *end high* concept would be defeated.

Right after training, don't involve your pet in another activity (including feeding, but do allow access to water), in order not to risk

*See chapter 9, "Training Session One."

distracting him after the fact. Rather than possibly override recent learning, encourage some quiet time for your pal to think about the previous lessons.

RULES OF TECHNIQUE

This notion is so important that it needs repeating: In any dealings with a dog you must operate at his level of understanding—it can't be brought to ours. No, I'm not suggesting you learn to howl at the moon or develop a taste for dog biscuits. I'm saying teaching must occur in a manner your dog can understand. Clearly, it's useless to say, "See here, dog—when I command, you obey!" Yet I've known otherwise sane people who expected results from essentially that approach.

Remember, the dog is the animal that turns around several times before lying down, to flatten grass and look for snakes—even when he's standing on a rug! He lives in a world far apart from ours, one he is permanently programmed into.

TEACH CLOSE

Lessons are best taught by keeping Pooch near you. That may seem obvious, but some training systems start with distance work. It's better to begin by teaching exercises like sit, lie down, and stay, with the dog close to you, then gradually increasing distance. To start at a distance is not only ineffective, it hampers bonding because it teaches that distance is part of the relationship.

ONE AT A TIME

Teach one lesson at a time. When teaching sit, for example, don't worry about where your dog sits. Some people teach the command while teaching the Heel position (facing forward at the handler's left side), but that attempts to teach two things at once. That's not only unwise, it's unfair. Dogs best learn only one thing at a time. This is especially true when starting schooling. That's when it's easy to confuse a willing animal by expecting him to master too much at once. Complicated work should be taught a step at a time. Practice recently taught lessons separately. For instance, if you taught heeling last week and lying down yesterday, today do a few minutes of heeling, *then* a few minutes of lying down.

Any two exercises can usually be practiced together after four to seven days of teaching the more recent element. The "If in doubt, don't!" rule applies because a main purpose of delaying the integration phase is to avoid stress.

TEACHING VERSUS POLISHING

Don't expect instant perfection. When teaching "lie down," for example, don't worry if Pooch lies on his side or back, instead of in an alert, straight position. It's better to teach approximates, polishing the work over time. In the long-term view of producing a reliable, happy worker, better a dog learn from success than from failure. Accept your pet's best attempts for what they are—his present best. He will do better with time and encouragement. Fine-tune as you go along.

FOCUS

During training keep your total attention on Pooch: It's the easiest way to capture his. As your dog should pay attention to you, teach by example—by maintaining your own concentration on your dog. If you're distracted by a clutter of unrelated thoughts, real training isn't happening. You aren't totally present at the situation because your mind is elsewhere. Your attitude must say there is you and there is your dog—nothing else matters at that particular time.

TIME OUT

Any animal can have an off day. If your dog has been doing well but one day he seems out of sorts, end the session with the intent of trying again the next day. For all you know, Pooch has a splitting headache.

EXCESSIVE REPETITION

Expect your pet to be getting the idea about any new lesson by the third or fourth demonstration. Slow learners exist, but dogs generally catch on quickly. The belief that your dog must be shown something hundreds of times is a myth. Such technique is understandably boring to you both. Worse, it can tell your pet he will never have to do the work himself; that you'll always help him along. Remember that in his natural setting, a dog might have only one learning opportunity. That's why nature has programmed him to soak up knowledge quickly.

GET IT RIGHT

When a dog blows an exercise he knows, repeat it quickly four to six times in a row with him making no major error. This helps him forget the incorrect response and allows successful completion of the work.

EASY DOES IT

Don't give a beginning dog commands you can't immediately enforce physically. If you've taught Pooch to "Sit!" near you, for example, don't jump to commanding "Sit!" at great distances. Without *gradually* increasing distance, your pet can learn to ignore not only commands but the sound of your voice.

IMPOSSIBLE SITUATIONS

As no living thing always does perfect work (people least of all, we should remember), any dog will blow any task if made to do it over and over and over. So don't work on any lesson for so long that what's really happening is your dog is being guaranteed a correction (punishment). That's not only stupid, it's cruel. Why? Because if a dog does as well as he's presently able, no prospect of improvement currently exists. To demand Pooch do better at a time when he can't do better is crazy-making.

BACK OFF

Should your dog have unusual difficulty with an exercise, let confusion fade by dropping the lesson for a few weeks. Then teach him via a different method and a *different-sounding* command. That's better than trying to fight through accumulated resistance to an old command. When replacing a command, *don't* link it in any way with the old word.

Similarly, if your dog isn't getting the idea via a given training method, try a different one. Watching trainers apply a technique for extended periods with zero results reminds me of a definition I once heard for insanity: doing the same thing and expecting different results.

INTEGRATION AND CONDITIONING

INTEGRATION

As stated earlier, this phase is practicing in sequence things your dog knows. It's similar to the way athletes and teams learn routines and plays.

WORK YOUR PAL FAST

Once training has progressed to the integration phase, work your pet quickly. I don't just mean you should walk hurriedly during heeling, for instance, but that you should go from exercise to exercise quickly. As one routine ends, praise and begin another. This kind of practice challenges a dog and heightens his enjoyment. It also captures attention—Pooch hasn't time for anything but you. Teaching a dog this working attitude also helps take him past contention: There's simply no time for him to make any objections he might have.

CONDITIONING

Conditioning is practicing integrated lessons in unfamiliar, increasingly distractive settings. Practicing while friends play nearby is a good distraction. Other good distractions are people, animals and busy locations. Don't use your pet's food dish, full or empty—that's unfair and can lead to pointless nervousness. Also, don't use a threatening or abnormally behaving person—it's foolish to put a dog in such a situation with the plan of smothering his protective instincts.

Don't use the dog's play toys as distractions; at least, not at first. That can lessen his attraction for the toys. In extreme cases a dog could even learn to distrust or fear the objects you use—or even you! Later, after your pet has had much practice, his toys can and should be used for distraction conditioning (requiring him to heel past a play toy, for example, to say your commands are what matters). But during initial training, keep your pet's toys removed from working sessions.

HERE AND THERE

Once you've started the conditioning phase, vary practice times and locations, working indoors as well as out and in all reasonable weather. It's neither necessary nor wise to train in subzero temperatures or at noon during a heat wave. Convincing Pooch that obedience is enjoyable—a program objective—can be difficult when he's freezing or tripping over his tongue. It is okay, though, to show him commands don't lose importance in a light rain or because it's nighttime.

COMMANDS

Commands tell a dog what to do. A command doesn't say just, "You should do this thing," but, "You *will* do this thing—now!"

It's one thing to teach a dog what a command means; it's another to say commands aren't open to a vote. A person can spend many training sessions showing what "Sit!" (for example) means in terms of an action; but until the trainer also conveys that this or any command additionally means, "You must!" it's unfair to hold the dog accountable.

In nearly all situations (I'll mention exceptions as we go along), give each command only once; not two, three or sixteen times. To repeat a command is to release the dog from responsibility. Besides, if Pooch didn't respond correctly the first time, he either couldn't hear you, is confused or just told you what he thinks about obeying.

Give your dog one clear, decisive command, with no hesitation in your next move. Indecisive commands result in lost rhythm and broken attention.

Don't use your dog's name with commands. The sound of the pack leader's voice provides all the keys a dog needs. The use of your pet's name is for when you and he are just spending time together, visiting, not for when you're working. A dog's mental processes are very fast, and to precede each command with his name is to let his attention wander. Pooch can learn he has enough time to let his mind drift, returning his focus to you during the time between the name and the command. Show your pet from day one that a single command is all he will hear, so his attention will stay where it belongs—on you.

A related idea is if commands are always preceded with the dog's name, he hears it so much his attraction to it is lowered; overuse can teach him to ignore its sound. Some people argue that using a dog's name when working is like saying, "Attention!" All that tells me is the dog's concentration is being lost between exercises.

Command only when you mean to. For instance, telling your pal when leaving the house, "*Stay here,*" lowers in his mind the significance of the command "Stay!" and the command to come to you ("Here!"). Why? Because while you're away your dog won't Stay (remain in one place), so he's being taught "Stay!" means, "Remain in one place, unless you think you can get away with moving." "Here" also becomes confusing, since your dog obviously can't come to you when you aren't there.

Communicate in your normal voice, so as not to threaten or beg rather than command. Only as you start to work at increasing distances or in crowded situations should you raise your sound level. When your friend is inches from you, speak normally.

PRAISE AND CORRECTION

"WHAT IF HE DIDN'T HEAR ME?"

This is an exception to the rule of giving a command only once. If you're working at a great distance in a noisy place and if Pooch couldn't hear you, of course you should repeat the command. The animal certainly shouldn't be punished as he couldn't have known there was something he was supposed to do. Too, don't pressure a dog that's confused or inhibited by a situation. He's just saying conditioning is coming along too fast. But if your friend is right next to you in a calm setting, and if he fails to respond to a command due to inattention, don't repeat the order—correct him.

TRAINING PURPOSES

Training is rooted in praise and correction. Either can support the other, as you'll see.

Praise teaches by giving a dog something he wants. It's used in two ways: To say Pooch did well, and when he can't be made to perform a given action. For example, a dog can be physically forced to sit, but he can't be forced to like it. That's where praise training comes in.

Correction is like punishment. It can be physical, spoken or both. It's used to teach a dog to avoid things that happen when he doesn't do as he's told.

PRAISE, CORRECTION AND CONSISTENCY

Praise and correction are two basic ways of allowing a dog to discover "where his own advantage or disadvantage lies."* With commands, praise and correction make up our basic language with dogs. Use each consistently so your friend can learn that his actions cause one to occur over the other. A person who trains inconsistently not only wastes time and effort, but confuses the dog.

Praise is affirmation. It's applause. It says "Yes, dog, that's right, and you did it very well!" It's petting calmly and gently while speaking quietly. Affection and acceptance aren't part of praise. True, they creep into the approval process, but both should be given a dog throughout his life. He shouldn't have to work for them.

Correction is pressure instantly applied for a disobedient act. It says, "You know that's not right." It's denial, not rejection; disapproval, not anger. Lower your voice during correction to prevent the act from becoming an emotional contest. A quiet voice makes a dog strain to listen, rather than concentrate on resisting.

Verbally praise according to what your pet just did, like "Good Sit," "Good Bring" and "Good Stay." This way Pooch hears the word again (for memory purposes) in the most positive tones you can use.

*Colonel Konrad Most, *Training Dogs: A Manual,* Popular Dogs Publishing Company, London, England, 1954, page 28.

Don't use praise words like "Good boy," "Good dog" or "Good Fido." The animal didn't do a *boy*, a *dog* or *himself*, so avoid confusion that can result from extra words. Besides, he's already a good dog. He always will be. That isn't to be decided from moment to moment. Remember: Praise (and correction) refer to a dog's *behavior*, not to the animal itself.

Avoid towering over your companion when praising, and don't pound on him when petting. Some folks say, "Oh, but he likes it." Watch his eyes sometime. The dog doesn't like it. It's learned to put up with it. Pet with a calm, gentle touch. Dogs feel such contact deeply. Pounding can bore, much as a consistently loud voice can lose importance, eventually to become ignored.

An effective manner of praise is, with the dog present, telling another person (preferably a family member) how well your pal just did some work. Keep your report simple, using only the animal's name, the commands he responded to and the praise word, "Good."

For instance, if your dog, Babe, did some particularly fine retrieving, you could walk the animal to a family member and excitedly say, "Babe, good bring!" Your human partner should enthusiastically reply, "Babe, good bring?" to which you respond, "Babe, good bring!" You could continue with, "Babe, good sit!" (an element of formal retrieving). Your helper should echo, "Babe, good sit?" to which you reply, "Babe, good sit!"

Use of the animal's name and of the commands coupled with "good" is half of this technique. Your approving tones and your helper's interest are the other half.

Extreme praise can actually frighten a sensitive animal; weakly praising a strong dog can cause distrust. Dominant dogs often react to gushy approval with, "I know I'm doing it well. You just hold up your end, sport!"

A similar notion is that for some dogs, praise can be lack of correction. For others, lack of praise can be correction.

Too much praise can break the moment. When overdone, it can actually distract from what you're trying to do. Once you've shown approval, get back to work. Like correction, praise should not be dwelled upon. Don't chop off the moment—let it fade.

CORRECTION: RULE #1

Here's as close as I'll get to giving you a hard and fast rule: *Never* use your pet's name during correction. He might misunderstand your meaning: believing that you feel *he's* no good, rather than his behavior is no good.

THE BASICS

One and only one reason justifies correction: contention—when a dog communicates, "I choose to disobey you!" Force is then right, communicating, "Think again!" In that sense correction is a teaching tool—it gives options. Mild, suggestive force is sometimes a teaching necessity, but using strong force to demonstrate a lesson is nothing less than abuse.

ASK THE RIGHT QUESTION

Though novices often ask how forcefully to correct, proper training should be concerned with "How quick?" before "How hard?" The best time to correct is when Pooch is a split-second into a disobedient act, when he's "thinking" about ignoring a command, so to speak. Correction (or praise) occurring more than two or three seconds after the fact is generally ineffective.

Besides, correction at the earliest moment requires less force. In the wild, a pack leader doesn't hesitate to flash his teeth when an underling starts to bring push to shove. The leader knows that's preferable to losing control. A quick setting of limits promotes harmony and cooperation.

THE RULE OF MINIMAL TOUGHNESS

In terms of sheer force, be one inch tougher than your dog, no more, no less. While trainers decide what is to be taught, dogs set the limits of how much force is needed. The lightest correction that does the job is the right one. A correction that is harder than needed can teach, yes, but what it teaches is fear of the trainer.

Build up on corrections, making them progressively tougher until you find what it takes to run your pet, then stay at that level. Better you should initially undercorrect than overcorrect. It's better to correct twice at first, while you're getting the feel of your dog, than it is to frighten through too much force. Remember, you can always get tougher.

Never correct a dog that's frightened or confused. The result is more fear or confusion. An upset dog will focus on survival as a priority, not learning. That's when corrections are abusive, teaching only fear and distrust.

Never correct a dog that's trying to do right. Otherwise a dog is taught to lose. The animal is told, "There's no point in trying." It also suggests a dog can or should perform any exercise perfectly from day one. Were that true, the word *practice* would have no meaning.

GET ON WITH IT

Don't dwell on a correction. Apply it quickly and move on. Grudges serve no useful purpose; patience, understanding, and forgiveness do.

Once you've determined what it takes to say to your dog, "Oh, yes you will!" (or "Oh, no you won't!"), don't back off from that degree of force. To undercorrect is cruelty, as it promises more and harsher corrections later. Underdone force makes a tough animal tougher.

Big doesn't imply tough; little doesn't guarantee gentleness. Big dogs can be softies, and little ones can dominate big ones with a glance.

MAKE IT CLEAR

Some trainers claim corrections should be made in silence. While that's proper at times, the silent correction method is a trap.

True, your pet can't understand every word you say, but he understands intent better if you speak your mind. Giving *brief* voice to your thoughts improves communication. Also, the day will come when you won't praise for every action—you don't want to spend your life praising for obedience learned years ago. So if corrections are always applied in silence, a dog can learn to feel nervous when there's no spoken praise.

Corrections should include as little handler movement as possible. Excessive motion can tell a dog you have difficulty handling him physically. With sensitive dogs, lots of handler motion can add fear to an otherwise instructive correction because some dogs are sensitive to sudden motion. Also, handler movements distract from the business at hand—the dog is more concerned with the movements than with the lesson.

A MYTH ABOUT CORRECTIONS AND PRAISE

Some trainers tie correction and praise together improperly. For example, a dog that knows "Sit!" doesn't respond to the command. The trainer corrects the animal and then immediately praises for sitting. The theory is this demonstrates the dog's choices—respond to command and be praised, or be forced to respond and then receive praise. This is one of those notions that works better on paper than in practice.

Approval should be given for things a dog does, not for things he's made to do. Praise is celebration, and it could seem to a dog that an after-correction "celebration" is due to his being punished. In this example, a more sensible sequence is as follows: The trainer says "Sit!"; the dog refuses; a correction is applied. Soon afterward the trainer moves the dog a few steps and again commands "Sit!" This time the dog sits and *this time* is praised. Praise now fits the response—it makes sense.

DON'T LOSE WHAT YOU'VE GOT

Sometimes a correction may seem right but is better skipped. Let's say you've been training for several minutes and your dog has been doing very well. Then his attention wanders for a second, resulting in a minor error. That's not the time to apply a physical correction. To do so would risk hurting his enjoyment of working with you. This is especially true for a dog that's been in training for only a few weeks. In this case it's better just to repeat the exercise so the dog can do it right.

Some folks disagree, demanding perfection at all times. I respect their sincerity if not their judgment. Such demands are unrealistic and are therefore unreasonable. No animal operates perfectly, and the notion of an "honest mistake" is realistic.

APPROPRIATE CORRECTIONS

When correcting a dog, be sure it's for the right reasons. For instance, let's say you're working Pooch near other dogs. If he attempts to lunge away for purposes of fight or play, the correction should include the message that the punishment is for breaking the command he was under, not for trying to go after another dog. If you command "Stay!" and your dog responds by jumping at another, correct yours for a broken Stay—tell him, "No! (pause for a second) Stay!"

The reason for this is it's easier for a dog to learn a positive than a negative. That's a normal part of canine nature, as dogs can better learn what to do than what not to do.

IMPROPER CORRECTIONS

Two so-called corrections have received much publicity in recent years. The first concerns striking an aggressive dog across his muzzle with a piece of rubber hose. Leave the hose in the garden where it belongs. Not only can such a blow cause head-shyness, it risks causing serious injury.

The second out-of-line correction is commonly referred to as "hanging the dog," which I've seen for sins no greater than slow sits. It's applied by literally holding a dog off the ground by the leash/choke collar until the animal changes his ways or passes out. Such "technique" is criminal abuse. It has no place in everyday training. Its only justifiable use is trainer protection, and even then only when there's no other out. I've used it as a defense three times since 1976, and each event was triggered by a dog that wanted—and that had the ability—to put me in the hospital.

PRAISE CORRECTION AND . . .

Deflection is a helpful technique for situations where neither praise nor correction seems right, but where some type of response is called for. Deflection is problem solving by ignoring low-risk problems or minor negative behavior to prevent either from worsening. The following story describes deflection's essence.

Some years ago, while helping position a student's Akita in the stand-stay (remain motionless in a standing position), the dog turned toward me and growled. I deflectively said, "The same to you," and continued with the business at hand, seeming to ignore him. I could have overpowered the dog and might have were he mine. However, the Akita is a breed that, like many, prefers one master, and this animal's resentment was on the order of, "Who do you think you are to be putting hands on me?" He simply did not appreciate a stranger's domination.

The point is that a dog has the right to choose the people he feels comfortable around just as you and I do. So long as a dog doesn't try to put teeth into his side of an issue, I deflect lesser signs of displeasure.

ADDITIONAL TIPS

Don't roughhouse with your pet, especially if he is of a larger breed. Doing so may seem harmless and cute during puppyhood, but later it can tragically backfire. Such "play" can send a message that fighting you is okay.

If your dog ever shows aggression toward you, back off. Get away from the animal and seek adult help. Don't *ever* confront a dog that is on the fight.

Don't laugh *at* a dog. That hurts him. Laughing *with* Pooch is fine, like when you're sharing an enjoyable moment, but never *at*. He's been provided for your amazement, not amusement. Those who ridicule a dog only reveal their distance from him.

Similarly, don't ask a dog questions. A pack leader doesn't ask; he or she directs. Besides, when you ask a dog something, his reaction can be nervousness, for three reasons. First, he's immediately put at a disadvantage: He can't participate. That is, do you honestly expect an answer? Second, you're saying you don't understand. For example, if your pet limps to you, he's already shown you what's wrong. Questioning your dog might suggest you have an incomplete grasp of the situation. Third, a questioning tone sends uncertainty. The dog is not helped by indecision; it only makes him more nervous.

Proper use of food is neither bribe nor reward. Once Pooch understands your commands must be obeyed, an occasional tidbit following a Recall ("Come to me," for example) is okay. However, present the snack not as a bribe but as a gift between friends: "Why, look what I just happened to find in my pocket—have some!" In the Recall example, your pet's reward is that coming to you allows him to be with you.

Remember there are few absolutes in dog training. Some things are merely more effective than others more often than not. A pro, regardless of his or her preferences as to what's right and wrong in the world of dog training, is flexible in approaching each dog. He or she does whatever it takes to produce a reliable, confident, happy worker.

This you may take to the bank: There is no perfect training method, no single correct or foolproof approach for teaching each and every dog each and every exercise.

That's why there are so many books on the subject. If there were an ideal method, there would be only one training text. This abundant variety is more proof that training is far more art than science. Those who claim, "My way is the only way!" are sort of boring.

REFLECTION

With enough practice . . . [these] skills will become second nature and your feelings of awkwardness will lessen. They will become part of your humanity rather than something tacked onto it.

GERARD EGAN

CHAPTER 8 TEACHING METHODS

When dog training is the issue, some instructors say that teaching is teaching, no matter the student's maturity level. Asserting that a trained dog is the objective regardless of the trainer's age, they approach the teaching of adults and children similarly. These instructors fail to recognize that while a trained dog is *an* objective, it's not the *only* one. Besides, kids and adults learn differently and as the training must suit the dog, teaching styles must suit the student. One-size-fits-all doesn't work.

DON'T WING IT

Plan your lessons, making sure you'll cover what students need to know to accomplish a given thing. Determine the basics of a given lesson so you can be sure to cover those elements.

OVERLOADED CIRCUITS

Present limited amounts of information at a time. Anyone's mental receivers/interpreters shut down when besieged by too much input. If you see an onset of glazed looks, back off. You can always cover finer points another time.

VOLUME

Speak loudly enough that you can be heard. Adults may say, "I can't hear you"; children usually won't. At the same time, don't overwhelm students with volume. Excessive decibels can inhibit.

ACT NOT

When instructors use baby talk, it can create distance. Children have less sophisticated vocabularies than many adults, true, but don't pitch your voice unnaturally because of your students' ages. Be yourself; be real. By the time they reach dog-program age, about eight years old,

One way an instructor can be heard is to stand within a circle of students.

most youngsters are poised enough to relate to adults and are understandably sick of being talked down to by them.

TECHNICALESE

Avoid technical language, especially with beginners. Everyday speech is suitable for our purposes. Using words students don't know means they won't understand what's being said.

IT'S SIMPLE, SO KEEP IT THAT WAY

Explore concepts to a lesser depth than if you were teaching adults; concentrate more on the *whats* than on the *whys*. Answer all questions, of course, but keep communication at a level students can handle. Besides, dog training is neither difficult nor complex, so keep it that way.

FACTS, NOT THEORIES

Whenever possible, use concrete lessons and examples; avoid explanations based on abstractions, especially with very young students. Successful communication via abstract concepts often hinges on common experiences and common perceptions. As children have had few adult-type experiences and are only just beginning to develop perceptions and outlooks, abstractions have a high potential to confuse or mislead.

COMMUNICATION AS AN ART FORM

Remember: You understand what you're saying in the way you're saying it, but that doesn't guarantee your students do. Kids sometimes smile and nod as though they comprehend everything being said when in reality they haven't the slightest idea of what's going on. They do this to be polite and agreeable, to "get along," one of many negative side effects of institutionalized, force-fed learning. See if your messages are getting through by asking students to explain them back to you.

SPEED

Teach children more slowly than adults, especially beginners. My first-session public obedience classes cover three commands; my 4-H First-Year obedience classes cover one. That doesn't imply adults are "smarter" than children—it recognizes that most youngsters have had little practice giving orders (commands). They've been on the receiving end but that's all. They need time to get used to being in charge. For many that's a major change, and since any change is stressful by definition, accelerated change is more so. Not incidentally, this slowed-pace teaching technique also acknowledges that most youngsters naturally have a shorter attention span than many adults.

I DID IT!

Format your lessons so students, especially very young ones, can rapidly achieve success. Yes, some things take time to refine, but an overall sense of having quickly achieved a goal is a potent confidence builder.

DIRECTNESS

Avoid subtlety. Be direct, clear. When showing students a judge's "Fast" heeling directive, for example, don't tell them to walk a little faster than quick, or to trot; tell them, "Run!"

PROMOTE THINKING

Encourage students to think. When introducing heeling, for instance, ask them what they think it is, then clarify. When a student's efforts aren't successful, don't reflexively point out the child is doing this or that wrong; ask the youngster what he or she thinks the problem is. Very often, if the instructor acts as a guide rather than an encyclopedia, the student leads him- or herself to the answer.

ENCOURAGE QUESTIONS

Make it easy for students to ask questions. Some kids hold back, for a variety of reasons, often thinking they'll "figure it out later." Of course, that means they don't understand it now.

SUPPORT

If you sense a student can do a given thing, let him or her know it too. If a child tries to answer a question but misses the mark, tell the youngster, "You're real close," not, "No, that's not right." Don't patronize or insult a student by saying something is right or well done when it isn't, but remove the sting by leaning toward positive aspects.

BEWARE OF BOREDOM

Repetition can be useful but don't overdo it. Tell students something once, then see if it took. Mentioning a certain training principle more than once is fine, but only as it relates to separate applications.

When you sense you do need to repeat an idea, put it in a somewhat different light. Say the same thing but differently.

STUDENTS AS TEACHERS

Have kids critique each other. For example, after several weeks of heeling practice, have each student heel for a few minutes while the group watches. After each youngster finishes, have the others say what they saw. This technique not only makes the watchers more aware, it gently accustoms everyone to being judged.

COLLABORATION

A similar procedure is having senior students help junior ones. Younger students are sometimes more at ease when taught by people closer to their own age, and the older kids quickly find out what they themselves know (as does anyone who teaches).

IT'S CALLED *REINFORCEMENT*

If you use written handouts, which I strongly recommend, review them for the class. Some kids learn better from spoken words than written ones. You don't need to read entire outlines aloud, but make sure everyone understands the gist.

THE SENSE OF SIGHT

Visual aids can greatly assist learning. Examples: Videotapes of students performing showmanship; a blackboard on which you might diagram a typical obedience ring setup; a large drawing of a dog with arrows pointing to various anatomical features.

BUILDING BLOCKS

Practice previous lessons. Sure, that's obvious, but I've known instructors to teach something and then not refer to it for several weeks. Regular review strengthens what has already been learned in students' minds.

DEMONSTRATE

This one's obvious, too, but it needs saying nonetheless: Describing an obedience exercise is fine, but demonstrate whenever possible. We can describe heeling, but demonstration works better for getting the idea across to your students.

EXPLAIN

Combine explanations with demonstrations. Just because a student sees you do something doesn't guarantee he or she understands it.

EXAM TIME

Whenever possible, "test" without students being aware that testing is occurring. You'll get more accurate readings. Some children have been taught to react apprehensively to the word *test*. Though they know the material, they have difficulty demonstrating their knowledge during a test.

YOU STARTED AS ONE, TOO

Last, know that children—especially very young children—sometimes have difficulty applying basic knowledge, particularly during pressure moments. I've seen beginners falter to the point of stumbling when distinguishing right from left when a judge directs, "Right turn," or "Left turn," during heeling. That's when compassion and empathy go a long way. It's certainly no time for impatience. It's when we do well to remember our own rocky road to adulthood, and that we're all in this together. As Emerson put it, "The secret of education lies in respecting the pupil."

APPLICATIONS

Applications of the foregoing techniques appear principally in section 4, "Obedience: First Year/On Leash" (chapters 9 through 17). All instances are referenced in the index.

REFLECTION

The essence of our effort to see that every child has a chance, to assure each an equal opportunity, not to become equal, but to become different—to realize whatever unique potential of body, mind and spirit he or she possesses.

JOHN FISCHER

OBEDIENCE: FIRST YEAR/ ON LEASH

9 TRAINING SESSION ONE

This section is meant to show students how to teach their dogs on-leash obedience, and to show instructors how to teach students. As effective teaching is rooted in how and in what order concepts are presented, my aim is to run several spoken-word "film clips" for you from a first-year/on-leash class series, so you might visualize the effects. The first lesson covers holding a leash securely.

LEASH GRIP

Hold your leash like this so Pooch can't yank it from your hand. Use whichever hand feels "right" and put your thumb through the loop of the leash and the loop's curve just behind your thumb's knuckle. Close your fingers around the loop, holding it, but not your thumb, in a fist.

While this leash-grip technique is useful in itself, it also allows students to learn something quickly and successfully. Many times when teaching this lesson I've heard variations on, "How about that!" and seen pleased smiles. The kids just learned something; they just entered the world of dog training.

MORE ABOUT LEASHES

The right leash is six feet long, and the lighter the better (but nothing the dog could break). Too heavy a leash can draw unwanted attention toward the equipment. Of course, that would hamper a basic goal— attracting the dog's attention toward the student.

Use either a leather, nylon or pressed-cotton leash; avoid chain. Chain leashes are not only rough on hands and legs, they are pointlessly heavy. They're also noisy, which lowers a dog's need to keep track

Correct leash grip.

of the trainer. Since Pooch can hear where the leash is—where his trainer is—the animal has less need to focus on number one.

WHAT'S THAT?

Next I select a well-known breed and ask the group, "What's that?" while pointing toward the dog and signaling the animal's young partner to remain silent. Occasionally some clown answers, "It's a dog." That's okay, the response usually gives everyone a chuckle, me included. It helps loosen things up.

"Very good! But what *breed* of dog do we have here?"

Pretty soon one of the kids identifies the animal and I pick another. We go through the class, one dog at a time, until each has been named. By now the youngsters are starting to relax, they're participating and most important, they're listening.

KEEP THE SMELLING SALTS HANDY

Because a trained dog is an objective, students have to see that training has its serious side, too. To suggest otherwise is dishonest. I introduce first-year trainers to reality by holding a medium-link pinch collar high enough that it can easily be seen and announcing, "People, this here is a pinch collar."

Silence.

"Most of you will need one."

Dead silence.

Some subjects are best approached head-on; pinch collar use is one such topic. This is an attention-grabbing, welcome-to-the-real-world moment, one that causes many students to react, perhaps not out loud, but with wide-eyed, nervous looks. To anyone new to training, a pincher's image can seem like a torture instrument. Nothing could be further from the truth, but how to demonstrate that to children whose main concern is their pet's welfare?

I know, it's a scary-looking gadget. That's because you're seeing the thing in people terms. "I sure wouldn't want one of those on me*!" Well, neither would I. But remember, we're training dogs here, not people.*

"Yeah, but I don't want to hurt my dog, either," you might think. Again, neither do I. So let me ask you something. Have you ever watched a mother dog discipline a pup? She grabs the little one's neck *with her* teeth *and the puppy calms down; Mom just said "I mean it!" Well, the purpose of a pinch collar is to put teeth on an animal that already knows what that feeling means—it's like Mom's teeth. The pup knew about that sensation when it was born; that kind of knowing is called an* instinct*—knowledge a dog is born with.*

Now, in every class there is at least one exuberant, large, canine powerhouse, one whose young handler is barely able to control. I approach them while speaking in a voice all can hear.

Tell you what: It's pretty obvious you've got a lot of dog there. Let me show you how this collar can make training easier for both of you. If you want me to take it off after a few minutes, I will. Fair enough?

As I near the dog, looking mostly at him, I'm aware he will probably try to jump on me. If he does, I deflect the problem by turning sideways and pushing the animal aside. I attach a pinch collar, hook my leash to the swivel (or the top ring if the collar has no swivel) and allow the dog to move away from me. He takes a step; I apply slight, one-handed leash pressure; the dog turns toward me; I easily guide him a few steps and the group is faced with a seeing-is-believing situation.

You see? This collar is "power steering," and I don't hear a dog screaming in pain, do you?

Now the children are seeing that a pincher isn't unkind after all; it's useful, humane training equipment. I return to the group and while petting the dog, bring the kids up to speed about a couple of training basics.

With practically every dog I train, I use a pinch collar. It's not only easier on me but more important, it's easier on the dog. Pooch knows that teeth-on-the-neck sensation forever. He respects it; nature tells him to. That's what I meant about an "instinct" a few minutes ago. Choke collars may "look" friendlier, but mostly they strangle. I mean, why do you suppose they're called "chokers" in the first place?

Let me tell you something about our best friend here. Dogs are pack animals. Do you know what that means? Well, what you and I call a family he calls a pack. All the training in the world won't change that—it can't. No dog will ever become some furry, four-legged type of human. For you to train your dog you have to become his pack leader: *Number one, the boss. That's who a dog* instinctively *respects and follows. And for you to become pack leader, you need to teach at your pet's level of understanding—he's the one being taught, so the lessons must be understandable to it. Pinch collar usage is a way to enter its world.*

After returning Pooch to his young partner, I go from dog to dog, putting a pinch collar on most.

FITTING A PINCH COLLAR

A loosely worn pinch collar is not only ineffective, it can come apart. Attach it snugly (though not really tight), so it appears to stand around the neck. Unlike the choker, pinch collar length can be adjusted by adding or removing links.

A pinch collar worn incorrectly (left) and correctly (right). Notice, too, the collar on the left contains too many links to be effective.

Notice you don't slide a pincher over your dog's head, like you would a choker. You wrap it around Pooch's neck and fasten it by hooking one link to another.

PINCH COLLAR SIZES

Pinch collars come in three link sizes: small, medium, and large. The larger the link, the greater the contact surface. The small collar is for dogs up to the size of a small Doberman. The medium-link size is for any other dog, except for the largest breeds, for which the large collar is appropriate. Should a dog be unaffected by the size recommended, use the next larger model.

Note to instructors: Though some dogs may cause you to think of recommending a large pincher, a medium may be more useful. Young people can have great difficulty attaching a large collar, as the leading link's prongs must be squeezed slightly together when attaching any pinch collar, and small hands may not have the needed power to compress the pronounced tensile strength of large links.

THEY'RE GREAT EQUALIZERS, TOO

"You mean you actually teach children it's okay to use a collar that looks like *that?*" Instructors reading this book may be faced with parents

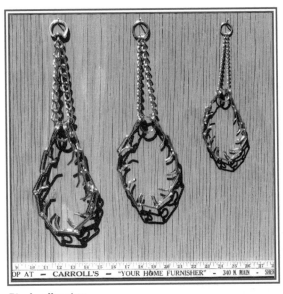

Pinch collar sizes.

asking similar questions. Seldom is a child hesitant to use recommend-ed equipment, but overly heltering moms and dads can be another story.

What a differ-ence a pinch col-lar can make! Using a cloth collar or even a tightened choker, this Basset Hound was nearly uncon-trollable. After a week of pinch collar training, however—well, see for yourself.

Of course, the answer to the question is "Yes," along with the com-ment that whether the dog is being trained by an adult or by a child, the point is that a dog is being trained, and that to reach the animal without undue violence a pinch collar is needed.

Besides, pinch collars allow some children to stay in the program with a dog they'd otherwise be unable to train. When there is, say, sixty pounds worth of kid and ninety pounds worth of rowdy, overactive dog with a neck like steel, there's no way the student can train the animal using a choker. An experienced trainer might be able to, but a begin-ning student can't.

The few youngsters who hesitate to use a pincher often ask, "Will it hurt my dog?" I answer, "If you mean injure, no. We aren't here to hurt dogs. You've got to be just a little tougher than the dog or it'll train you. That's how dogs are. If you don't become *pack leader*, the dog will. He has to."

A final question is whether instructors should sell pinch collars. I do, for the simple reason that I can make sure the collar is properly sized and fitted.

A WORD OF CAUTION ABOUT COLLARS AND AGGRESSION

Training collars—pinch or choker—can trigger an aggressive response, especially when used with so-called fighting breeds. A closable collar on the "wrong" dog can fire an attack almost before you can blink. We've had mercifully few such dogs in our local program, and have dismissed them from class, as there's simply too much risk to the kids.

I spend a few minutes with the "exuberant, large, canine powerhouse" after putting a pinch collar on him because if the dog is going to respond with fire, better he do so with me. Most dogs telegraph their intentions and, like any good trainer, I'm familiar with such warnings, I know how to protect myself and can usually stop the problem permanently. Understand, if the trouble is rooted in bad breeding, I won't get any further with the dog than anyone else would. But if aggression does occur, which is rare, it's usually a doggy version of, "I wonder if I can get away with this?" Once that question has been successfully settled, the dog usually changes his ways for all time.

If confronted by a determined fighter—one that can and will attack, not just nip, anyone who tries to dominate him via leash and collar—regardless of the dog's size, the first rule is to protect yourself, leash-jerking the animal onto its back legs if need be to keep him off you. Then hand the lead to the child's parents and advise them Pooch isn't right for the program, which such a dog clearly isn't. Even though you may be able to handle the animal, he's too dangerous to have around children.

SIT

PICK THE RIGHT DOG

First I select a dog to demonstrate teaching "Sit!" I look for one that's attentive, relaxed and interested in the proceedings. He's easy to spot: He seems to be studying me and doesn't flinch from a few seconds of eye contact. Once I've picked a dog, I ask the youngster if I may briefly borrow the animal.

DON'T TURN YOUR BACK

I take the leash and walk backward, away from the dog, while patting my leg, saying, "C'mon, pup," and keeping my attention on him. The walking backward technique is to attract Pooch without force—most dogs will follow a person who's walking backward. Should I turn my back to the animal, I risk emotionally blocking him, causing him to resist going with me. With the *wrong* dog I also risk being bitten by taking my eyes off him. Besides, I'll be telling the students often during the next few weeks to keep their attention on their dogs, so I exemplify the point from day one.

TRAINING PRINCIPLE NO. 1

As I stop and allow the animal a moment to sniff and check me out, I introduce a training basic.

People, there's something you have to know: It's one thing to teach a dog what a command means, but it's another to show the dog he has to do it, that your commands aren't open to a vote. We can show this fine animal any number of times what "Sit" means in terms of a specific action, but no real training can happen until we also say, "And by the way, dog, you have to do it." That's sort of what obedience is—the dog minding regardless of whether he wants to.

Now, let me tell you what you're going to see. First, I turn the collar so the chain part is at the front of the neck. Then I'll move Pooch so that while he may not be looking right at me, he'll be facing toward me. Once your pal is in position—standing and facing generally toward you—command "Sit!" and a half-second later leash-pull him so close to you that he almost touches you. Listen, now—I said pull, *don't jerk the leash. As you pull, keep your hands togeth-*

The first step in teaching "Sit!": Maneuver the dog so she is looking in your direction.

The finished product, sort of. A purist might push this trying-to-please dog's foot away, but to me that would just be a good way to dampen spirit.

Step two in teaching "Sit!" Upwardly directed leash pressure toward the handler causes nearly any dog to sit. Note that only minimal force is needed, even with this adult Labrador Retriever.

er and close to your body, at a level just a little higher than your dog's head. The whole thing should take less than two seconds. Relax your leash the second your dog sits, take the pressure off him and praise "Good sit, good sit!" You got all that? Okay, watch.

The next thing the youngsters see is a sitting dog. I briefly praise the animal "Good sit!" while petting it under the chin, to teach him to sit and look at the trainer. I move Pooch with, "C'mon, pup," and quickly repeat the lesson. By the fourth time, most dogs sit before leash pressure can be applied.*

There! See how quickly this fine dog got the idea? He did that last sit on his own, without any leash pressure. Note that was when I really laid on the praise, "Good sit!" Now, I'm going to return your dog to you, he's a nice one, and what I want you guys to do for a few minutes is teach "Sit!" Move away from each other; get some room between yourselves. Teach "Sit!" Get your dog facing you, command, "Sit!" and pull your lead; not too hard, now. Praise the dog when he sits, then move him and do it again. Holler at me if you have a problem. Don't forget to relax your leash as your dog sits.

TAKE FIVE

After a few minutes I call the group together.

People, you're doing really well. But I hear some of you making a common mistake: repeating, "Sit!" Don't worry, new adult trainers do it, too. But tell your dog once, *then make him sit.*

Notice we don't use the dog's name with commands. He knows whom you're talking to, and we want to teach him that one command is all he'll hear, so he'd best pay attention.

Okay, work on "Sit!" a little longer.

REVIEW

After the kids have practiced "Sit!" for five or six minutes, I call them together for the final time that day.

You're doing good, guys. I think this class is going to do okay and have a lot of fun, too. Now, what are we working on this week? That's right, "Sit!" Questions?

---

*Experienced trainers quickly discover that my method of teaching sit requires surprisingly little force, far less than the conventional push-pull style (pushing down on the dog's rear while pulling upward on the leash). A thorough outline of the technique's rationale appears in my book *Dog Logic: Companion Obedience.*

One I occasionally hear is, "My dog sits better if I touch him on the butt when I say, 'Sit!' Is that okay?"

Answer: Sure—if it works, use it.

After distributing the week's written material, I review it with the class, ask once more for questions and end the session.

CHOKE COLLARS

All students will need a choker for showing Pooch: A dog cannot be shown in a pincher. The proper size for a choker is the distance around the dog's neck plus two inches. Link size depends on the dog's size: large for the largest breeds, medium for those in the Labrador range, small for spaniel types and very small for those tinier than a small Sheltie.

A choke collar is worn so the *live ring* comes over the top of the neck toward you when Pooch is at your left side. The *live ring* makes the collar tighten; it's what you attach a leash to, so the collar loosens when a tightened lead is relaxed. The other ring is called the *dead ring*.

A choke collar worn incorrectly (left) and correctly (right).

[NAME OF COMMUNITY] DOG TRAINING PROJECT

SOME TRAINING HINTS

Work daily with your dog for ten to fifteen minutes, but not sooner than an hour after feeding him. Give him a chance to relieve himself before work or play begins.

If you work with your pet for fifteen minutes a day, you should play with him for at least fifteen minutes a day. Keep play time separate from work time for now. Have him wear the training collar during either activity, but give *no* commands during play periods.

Remove any toys from the dog's sight after play. If a toy is left to lie around, its attraction to the dog lessens greatly; it loses its magic.

Don't use play objects as distractions. Some good distractions are other animals, people and busy locations.

Teach new lessons in a distraction-free area. Gradually add distractions only after learning has taken place.

Family members may be allowed to watch practice sessions, but should not speak the dog's name or make eye contact with him.

Carefully plan each training period, anticipating how your dog is likely to perform and how you'll respond.

Give *one* clear, decisive command and proceed, with absolutely no hesitation in your next move.

Use commands only when you mean to, and don't give a command you cannot immediately back up physically.

The dog's name is not used with commands; it's sometimes used during praise; it's *never* used during correction.

The time for effective training is not when either of you are tired or ill, or when you are hurried for time or are irritated.

Praise your dog according to what he has just done, like "Good sit," "Good bring" and so forth; not "Good boy," "Good dog" and the like.

Avoid looming over your dog when praising him, and don't pound on him in affection. Pet calmly and speak quietly, communicating approval rather than affection. Affection should be given to a dog throughout his life— he shouldn't have to work for it.

Don't work at any one thing for such a long time that what you're doing is guaranteeing your dog a correction. That teaches an animal to lose.

Vary the times and locations of your practice sessions, working indoors as well as out, and in all reasonable weather.

End each period on a positive note, with the dog having just done an exercise right and being praised.

Don't involve your pet in any other activity (including feeding, but make sure he has water) immediately after training. Better he should have some quiet time.

Your dog can have only one trainer: you.

Inappropriate aggression from a dog is not to be tolerated, ever.

Never allow an unsupervised dog to wear any collar!

[NAME OF COMMUNITY] DOG TRAINING PROJECT

OBEDIENCE I WEEK I

Training Exercise	Command	Per Session	Foundational or 7-Day Objective
1) Sit on Command	Sit	8 to 10	Dog's attention & comprehension

SIT ON COMMAND

Get your pet facing you by walking backward. With your hands a little higher than your pet's head, command "Sit!" and leash-pull (don't yank) him so close he nearly touches you. This makes him sit. As the dog sits, relax your leash and praise, "Good sit!" while petting him under his jaw. After a few seconds, tell your pal, "C'mon," and walk backward to move him a little so you can repeat the lesson.

Good luck!

REFLECTION

A problem is a chance for you to do your best.

DUKE ELLINGTON

TRAINING SESSION TWO

Guys, I'd like for you to move your dog a couple of feet—tell him, "C'mon, Pooch," or some such—then stop and command, "Sit!" Let's see how you're getting along. Okay? Have at it.

I ask the class to perform the "Sit!" enough times so that I can see how each team is progressing. One or two dogs usually haven't gotten the word that obedience doesn't allow for, "If I feel like it."

Okay, some of you are still having to say, "Sit!" several times before your dog does it. We have to get past that, or we don't have obedience. Let me show you how.

For instance, this dog here has his own ideas about whether he needs to sit when he's told. Does that make him bad? Or dumb? Of course not. It just means he doesn't know the rules yet. Tell you what: If I can have your leash for a minute, let me show you what to do. C'mon, pup. I walk the animal a few steps, then, Sit!

What happens next is the dog ignores me as he did his young owner and I leash-jerk the pooch into a sit. Then I move him a few paces and again command, "Sit!"; this time the reluctant canine obeys. While praising, "Good sit!" I ask the group what will become a routine question at these classes: "What did you see?"

REVIEW MATERIAL

Sit

NEW MATERIAL

Heeling
Automatic Sit

After a brief hesitation, someone speaks up. "You said "Sit!" yanked the leash and the dog sat."

"Right. I yanked upward, slightly toward myself. Then what?"

"You walked him some more and told him to sit again, and he did."

"What did I do then?"

"You petted him and said 'Good sit!'"

Sure. I'm giving the animal a choice: He can sit when he's told and be pet-ted, or he can be jerked into a sit—it is up to the dog. I'm making the dog's behavior his *responsibility, as it should be. You have to answer for what you do, don't you? Well, so should your dog.*

Now, how hard do you yank the leash? That depends on a couple of things. First, how big is the dog? This German Shepherd I'm working with weighs about eighty-five pounds. But that Toy Poodle over there—well, if I yanked his leash as hard as I did the Shepherd's, the Poodle might wind up on the roof. So size is a factor in determining how hard to yank.

The other factor is toughness—how tough is your dog? Let me tell you some-thing: Pound for pound, that Miniature Schnauzer over yonder is the toughest dog here. If he were the size of this Shepherd, much force would be needed to make him do anything.

Now, the danger is correcting too hard, not too softly. So when you first cor-rect your pet, start gently. You can always yank the leash harder the next time if you have to. If you yank too hard to start with, you may frighten the dog rather than "train" him.

Here's your pooch back; he's sure a neat dog. I want you guys to move your dogs one more time. Tell them, "C'mon, dog," or something like that. Then stop and command, "Sit!" Make them sit if they don't obey. If your dog sits, just praise him; don't jerk the leash. But if Pooch doesn't sit after one command, yank the lead like I showed you; make that critter sit. Teach that whether or not you jerk the leash is up to the dog; if he does as he's told, he'll be petted. If he doesn't, well. Okay, do it.

This is a very important moment in terms of student safety. If I have the slightest suspicion a dog may respond to force by becoming aggres-sive toward the youngster, I briefly work the dog myself, getting him past whatever problem he has with being pressured into submission. Otherwise, I watch the group—two or three adults are helping at this point—and if any dog shows hostility, the nearest adult quickly takes the leash and gets the dog properly focused. After a few minutes, I fur-ther clarify a point.

You see, people, that's what obedience training is: showing a dog what you want, then giving him a choice. He can do what you tell him to and be praised, or you'll make him do it. It's up to the dog. Okay, who's got questions?

The sit correction, applied to two markedly different dogs.

Note to instructors: If you have to work a potentially aggressive dog, here is a relatively safe way to physically praise the animal. Your left forearm near the dog's neck and head provides something of a barrier should Pooch turn and snap, and allows you a chance to react by pushing the dog away.

Frequent questions at this point are:

Q. "What if my dog didn't hear me?"
A. "Don't correct him—talk louder when you give commands."

Q. "What if I jerk my leash and he still doesn't sit?"
A. "Jerk the leash harder."

Q. "How long do I wait to yank my leash?"
A. "About a second. You have to give Pooch time to respond; but if you give him too much time, he won't learn he has to do what you tell him right away."

Q. "Do I pet my dog after I jerk the leash?"

A. "Nope. Move him a few steps; command, "Sit!" again, and *this time* pet him, assuming he obeys. You only praise a dog for what he does, not for what you must make him do."

Occasionally, a youngster needs more guidance about, "How hard do I jerk my leash?" A good way to communicate the notion is by involving the student's sense of touch along with sound and sight. I ask the child to grasp the loop end of the leash, holding it tightly; and I jerk the lead hard enough to get the idea across, but not so severely as to risk injuring the student.

People, you and your dogs are doing well. You're on a roll. Let's keep it going by getting into heeling.

HEELING AND AUTOMATIC SIT

HEELING DEFINED

"Here's a question for you guys: What's heeling?"

"It's telling your dog to take a walk with you."

That's a good answer, but there's a little more to it. First, the dog stays in the same place compared to where you are. He doesn't walk on your right side sometimes and your left side other times; he doesn't walk ahead or behind you; he's always at the same place, next to your left leg. Also, when you stop, he sits automatically, without command, and right next to you. Let me show you what I mean.

I ask an advanced student to heel his or her dog on leash while the class watches. (Earlier I spoke with the student, so as not to hit the youngster cold with the notion of "performing.") After a few minutes I thank the student, return to the group and ask two questions.

Get the idea? Good. So how do you teach heeling and automatic sit?

Blank stares are commonplace at this point.

Okay, look at it this way. When you take your dog for a walk on leash, does he ever try to pull you along?

Now there are chuckles and affirmative nods of first-hand experience.

Sure, because when you pull a dog one way, he often pulls the other way. We used that to our advantage last week when we taught the sit, remember? You pulled your leash toward yourself; your dog reacted by trying to pull the other way and that made him sit. So pulling on the leash isn't going to work to teach heeling, is it? If anything, that would work against you—it would make your dog pull away from you. Let me show you how to teach heeling.

I seek out the "exuberant, large, canine powerhouse" mentioned in the previous chapter, ask the owner if I can borrow Pooch for a couple

Two views of the heel position.

of minutes and demonstrate the basics of teaching heeling and automatic sit.

Okay, watch what happens. First I command, "Sit!" Now the dog is sitting and I'm praising, "Good sit!" Then I stand next to his right shoulder; it's next to my left leg. This is the heel position.

Now, let me tell you what's going to happen so you can watch for it. I'm going to tell Pooch to heel and start walking. Depending on how he reacts, I may pat my left leg to help him get the idea of what I want. If this dog is like many, he'll come along for a step or two and then wander off, trying to pull me along. At that instant I'll turn and go the other way. Watch.

After a few minutes of walking north whenever the dog goes south, and of teaching the animal about automatically sitting as I stop (I'll tell you how shortly), I return the dog to his owner and ask the youngsters, "What did you see?"

"Well, when he went away from you, you went the other way."

"Right. Then what happened?"

"The dog ran to the end of the leash and then turned around and came with you."

"Sure. I was saying to him, 'Hey, Pooch, it's your neck. If you want to hit the end of the leash, I'll let you; but the days of dragging me along are over.' In other words, I made him responsible for his own behavior, like I did with 'Sit!' I gave him a choice. Now, what did I do when I stopped walking?"

"You said, 'Sit!'"

"And made Pooch do it if he didn't obey. What about the last three times I stopped walking?"

"You didn't say, 'Sit!' but he did anyway."

"Sure—he was learning the pattern: 'We stop, I sit.' Let me work with another dog for a few minutes, so you can see the process once more."

After selecting a second dog, I continue demonstrating how to teach heeling and the automatic sit. I haven't told the kids everything they need to know yet; I'll pass along some more information after working the second dog. Telling students too much during a brief time almost guarantees they'll misunderstand much of it, or forget it altogether.

After finishing with the second dog, I ask, "Does it look a little more familiar now?" This usually results in nodding heads because the kids knew what to expect and saw it.

"Okay, let me ask you something: What command am I using for heeling?"

Often the answer is, "I couldn't hear you."

No, you probably couldn't. That's because I don't believe in yelling commands when the dog is close to me. That can make a dog stop listening. The word I used is, "Fuss!" It's a German word, and it rhymes with loose and means "foot." I don't use "Heel!" because when I teach the dog to come to me, which we'll do in a few weeks, I use "Here!" and that sounds too much like "Heel!" Words that sound like other words are hard for a dog to learn.

Now, there's one other thing I'm doing when I'm teaching heeling. When I start walking I start with my left foot. It's nearer to Pooch and he can more easily see I've started moving.

Okay, find some room—put some distance between each other—and teach your dog heeling and automatic sit. Teach "Fuss!" Don't forget to say, "Sit!" when you stop walking.

After watching the youngsters for a few minutes I call them together.

People, I have one last thing to tell you. You've been saying, "Sit!" when you stop walking. Sometime soon your dog will sit automatically when you stop walking; he'll learn the pattern. The first time he does sit automatically, drop the "Sit!" command. Why? Because it's obvious he's getting the idea—taking your stop as a signal to sit. If you keep saying "Sit!" Pooch might think he's missed the lesson, that he needn't auto-sit because you'll always say, "Sit!"

The first time your pet auto-sits is important. Praise him to show that the auto-sit is what you've been after. Look at your pet, send a message that you're pleased—"Well, now! Look at you!"—let him know you've seen what he's done and praise him! Let your pet know you appreciate what he just did; it was right and you're proud of him.

After the first time Pooch auto-sits, correct him anytime he doesn't sit automatically. Keep praising, "Good sit!" for awhile, though. You'll use "Sit!" with other lessons, and even quick learners must hear a word a lot to lock the sound into mind. Questions?

One way to keep your dog's attention on you is to keep yours on him.

Then I have the group practice heeling for a few minutes, distribute the week's written material and close the session.

[NAME OF COMMUNITY] DOG TRAINING PROJECT

OBEDIENCE I WEEK 2

Training Exercise	Command	Per Session	Foundational or 7-Day Objective
1) Heel on Leash	Fuss	8 to 15	Dog's attention

HEELING AND AUTOMATIC SIT

Begin with Pooch sitting squarely at your left side. This is the *Heel Position*. Look at your dog, command, "Fuss!" and walk a few steps, starting on your left foot. As you stop, command, "Sit!" Praise, "Good sit" as you pet under the chin.

Once a dog understands a command, he becomes responsible for it. So as soon as your pet begins to auto-sit whenever you stop walking, stop using the "Sit!" command. Continue to praise, "Good sit!" though, to let your pal know you appreciate his good work

---

REFLECTION

Always listen to experts. They'll tell you what can't be done and why. Then do it.

ROBERT HEINLEIN

11

TRAINING SESSION THREE

HEELING PROBLEMS

SLOW STARTS AND LAGGING

If your companion starts late or lags behind, correct the problem now. Get Pooch in the heel position and hold the leash right-handed at waist level with slack hanging slightly below your left knee. With your feet together, allow yourself to tip forward. Just before the moment when you must take a step to keep from falling over, command, "Fuss!" and shoot your left leg forward. It will strike the leash. If your pet starts with you, he'll receive no correction. If he starts late, one or two applications of this technique should cure the problem.

If your pet starts okay but lags once you're moving, hold your leash as described. Your left leg will hit the lead as you walk. If Pooch stays next to you he will receive no correction. If he drops behind, the method should bring him along quickly.

Be aware these practices are *not* for small dogs relative to the physical size of the handler. Were they used with a Yorkshire Terrier, for instance, the force of the leg striking the lead might toss the Yorkie into the next county. For small animals a sharp, left-handed motion with or into the leash does the job, but with less force and less risk to the dog.

"BUT I ITCH, YOU SEE"

Another type of lagging occurs when a dog decides to stop and scratch for whatever reason. Keep walking. Your commands are what count. Besides, if Pooch learns he can stop you, either by scratching, yawning, stretching, shaking or in any other way, then the question becomes, "Who is heeling whom?"

THE CALL OF NATURE

"But what if my dog stops to go to the bathroom?"

That, too, he can learn to take care of during his off hours. It's another type of lagging. Keep going. If you ever *need* to move your dog hurriedly from one place to another, you won't want to wait for him to first take care of his body's business.

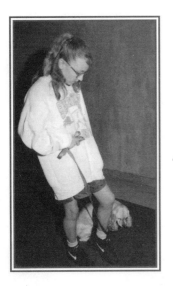 

To cure the slow start.

FORGING AHEAD

To correct the forger, merely stop walking. The animal will blow the automatic sit because he will be out of position; he will be ahead of you. As you stop, immediately leash-yank Pooch slightly behind you, then tug him forward into the heel position.

To the dog that decides he can dominate the situation by hurriedly backing into position as you stop, wish him lots of luck! He will discover that your alertness led to starting the correction before he could even begin to scoot back.

THE LEANER

If your companion leans against you, don't correct him until he's had enough training so you're sure he won't see your reaction—brushing him away with the side of your knee or foot, depending on his size—as rejection. Correcting too soon could cloud your messages—merely wanting your own space, and that your dog doesn't need you (or anyone else) to prop him up, physically or emotionally. Don't risk telling a young or nervous dog he's not wanted, or that his touch offends.

Once correction is appropriate, if stubbornness is Pooch's reaction—where a bump causes glaring and pressing harder—the situation has changed and so should your response. One or two collar blasts leftward, along with, "No! Sit!" ("Sit!" also means, "without leaning against me"), usually gets the meaning across. Then heel a few steps and praise, "Good sit!" as the dog shows you by sitting without leaning that he understands.

CROWDING

The leaner's cousin is the crowder, the dog that insists upon riding against your leg during heeling. This happens mostly with large dogs.

If the animal is touch-sensitive, the cure may be carrying the leash left-handed, so it hangs between your leg and Pooch. A sensitive dog avoids brushing against a lead. If this has no effect, correct with a series of bumps to the neck area with your knee as you walk, coupled as needed with outward leash yanks. As the dog begins to heel properly, praise, "Good fuss!"

HEELING WIDE

Opposite of the crowder is the dog that heels wide to the left. If you think your pet's problem is fear-based rather than disobedience, as can happen with a new animal with a history of abuse, soft words and patting your leg are the best answer. If the problem has its roots in stubbornness, a series of right turns often brings a dog into line. If it doesn't, use right-handed leash pops toward yourself, adding, "No! Fuss!" as you walk. Praise, "Good fuss!" as your dog heels properly.

CROOKED SITS

A common heeling problem is the crooked sit. By crooked I don't mean a sit that's off-line by a sixteenth of an inch, so to speak. I don't call sits that closely and you shouldn't, either.

Every trainer has a personal definition of the line between a straight sit and a crooked one. My rule is that if my pet heels in position and sits squarely and in rhythm as I stop, and doesn't push himself away or lean against me, I'm happy.

The crooked sit can lead to real problems and can be seen in a dog that sits at a right angle to the handler. The dog that sits that crookedly will generally wind up sitting in front of you. Eventually he won't sit at all.

Here are two basic solutions. With an inexperienced dog, practice as much as possible next to walls, fences and similar things to your left, making other than straight sits impossible—no room is left for Pooch to swing his butt away. This can teach the proper habit.

With the dog that requires sterner measures, yank him behind and slightly to your left, then jerk him forward into position. Quickly heel a few paces and stop, to see if your message got through. Praise if you succeeded, but if more force is needed, so be it. Keep in mind that this seldom-needed correction is only for dogs whose attitude is, "Make me!"

MORE ABOUT HEELING

*There's something about heeling I didn't mention last week. I told you to start on your left foot, yes? Well, you should stop on your **right** foot. As you stop, don't swing your left foot past your right to take another step. This teaches a smooth, glide sit because it's easier for Pooch to see that you're stopping. He sees that the leg closer to him has stopped and he sits. Try it a few times—heel your dogs around and stop on your **right** foot.*

In addition to letting students practice the new procedure, I'm seeing how heeling has fared during the week but without letting them know it. Kids often do better when they don't feel the pressure of being "graded." After a short time I call them together.

You guys are getting the idea real well. This class is the kind that makes an instructor look good. Now let me ask you something. You know when to praise for sitting—you say "Sit!" the dog sits, you praise—right? But when do you praise for good heeling?

Someone usually says, "When your dog is walking with you."

That's a very good time. Another is as your dog takes his very first step with you. You say, "Fuss!" your dog moves from the sit—that's when he's really doing something. Or when you make a turn and the animal fights to stay with you. Again, that's when he's really working at heeling. Now, don't stop walking to praise or you'll be saying, "Good fuss!" to a dog that isn't moving, and that's confusing. Keep moving as you praise, and if your dog is tall enough, pet him as you say, "Good fuss!" Try it for a few minutes. Heel your dogs and praise them when they're doing good. Don't say, "Good fuss!" over and over; once or twice per command is enough. Go ahead.

While the students practice I watch to see which dogs have learned the automatic sit, which is the next element to look at.

Okay. You're getting this "Good fuss!" business. Now, how many dogs are doing auto-sit at heel? Show me some hands. Okay, everybody wait here a minute.

I go to the parents and ask for four "volunteers." I position each parent about thirty feet apart so they form the corners of a square. Then I fill in each side of the square with kids and their dogs.

Do you see the outlines of the square we've made? Our parent-helpers are the corners. Here's what we'll do: When I say, "Forward," you command "Fuss!" and start walking. Turn when you get to a corner, and when I say, "Halt," stop walking and praise, "Good sit!" if Pooch sits. Correct him if he doesn't. We'll go clockwise. Don't run into the dog ahead of you. Ready? Forward!

After letting the group walk halfway around the square I direct, "Halt," and note which dogs sit automatically.

Okay, the Greyhound, the Miniature Schnauzer and the Doberman all sat. You guys bring those dogs into the center of the square, next to me. Everyone else: This time when you stop, if your dog doesn't sit, correct him. Forward!

I maintain this routine for several minutes, pulling out dogs that auto-sit and letting youngsters whose dogs aren't getting the idea keep at it until each dog sits automatically. Then we move on to "Stay!"

SIT-STAY

Real good, guys. They're getting the auto-sit fine. Thanks, parents. Now let's teach "Stay!"

TEACHING THE SIT-STAY

Start with your pet sitting at heel. Your leash should be in your left hand and have very little slack. Now all at the same time, give the stay signal—your right hand a few inches in front of your dog's nose—command "Stay!" and step away one long pace and turn and face the animal. Silently count to five, return to the heel position and praise, "Good stay!" while petting your dog under his chin. Try it once. Command, "Stay!" and move off.

Teaching the sit-stay.

Slowly increase time and distance over the next few days. By next week you should be six feet away for a minute.

WHAT IF MY DOG MOVES?

Say, "No!" and leash-correct him back to where he was; don't just guide him back—jerk the leash.

Watch your pet closely. You'll need less force if you can catch him when he's one blink into movement, when he's just started to move. Very little force—often just, "No!" and a leash flick—is needed then. So don't be in a hurry to get far away. Take your time. You can always get farther away.

VERBAL BRIDGE

The reason for telling the dog, "No!" right away if he moves during a stay is to show him exactly where he went wrong. He didn't goof because he went this or that direction; it was because he moved. The "No!" is because you may be some distance away, and by the time you get to your dog to correct him, enough time may have passed by that he might not understand what he did wrong. Saying, "No!" as he moves shows him where he messed up.

STAY PROCEDURES

Guys, when you're teaching "Stay!" make it easier for your dog by leaving on your right foot. It's farther away from him and its movement is less likely to pull him along. Remember: Start heeling with your left foot, start a stay with your right.

WHAT IF MY DOG LIES DOWN?

Immediately say, "No!" and leash-lift him into the sitting position. Then leave again for a short time, so he can successfully complete the stay.

Now let's try a sit-stay again—leave your dogs.

After this second sit-stay we end the session.

You guys and your dogs are doing really well. Stay with it. Next week it gets easier. Here are this week's sheets. Thanks for coming and good luck!

[NAME OF COMMUNITY] DOG TRAINING PROJECT

OBEDIENCE I WEEK 3

Training Exercise	Command	Per Session	Foundational or 7-Day Objective
1) Heel on Leash	FUSS	8 to 15	Dog's attention & comprehension
2) Sit-Stay	STAY	3 to 6	Sit for 1 minute

SIT-STAY

Start with your dog sitting at heel, and with the leash in your left hand; there should be very little slack. At the same time, put your right palm in front of your dog's nose, command, "Stay!" and step forward on your right foot a long pace, turning to face your pet. After a few seconds, return to the heel position and praise, "Good stay!"

Each day increase the time and distance with the goal of six feet for one minute by next week, but no more than that. Once you're able to be away from Pooch for more than just a few seconds, move around rather than standing in one place.

REFLECTION

If you think you can or think you can't, you're right.

12

TRAINING SESSION FOUR

DISTRACTIONS

Let's talk for a few minutes about distractions. It's a big thing in dog training.

I bet every dog here does better obedience work at home. At home, other dogs and people aren't around, like they are here. They are distracting your dogs from what they're supposed to be doing—listening to you. So we need to get into distraction training, so your pets can learn to listen to you, not to things going on around them. Otherwise, whenever you're around another dog, or people or whatever grabs your pet's attention, his obedience will go right out the window.

The idea is to work Pooch around distractions, praising him when he listens to you, correcting him when he doesn't. That doesn't mean you should practice around anything that's scary to him, but maybe while a couple of your friends are playing catch, or are working their dogs. Get the idea?

So one thing you'll work on during this week is training around distractions. For now let's set up one of our own. Half of you guys line up next to each other, about six feet apart, on one side of the yard, the rest of you line up on the other side. That's right, this puts about forty feet between your two groups. Now the group on that side, face the group on the other side, and vice versa. Okay, here's what

REVIEW MATERIAL

HEELING AND AUTOMATIC SIT

SIT-STAY

NEW MATERIAL

DISTRACTIONS

(LIE) DOWN-STAY

Traffic heeling. Figure eights are a breeze for dogs that can handle this type of conditioning.

we're going to do. When I tell you, both groups are going to heel to the other side of the yard; where the other group is now, and turn to face where you came from.

As the message dawns, I begin hearing from my students everything from giggles to exclamations of, "Oh, no!"

That's right, you're going to pass each other when you near the center of the yard. More important, your dogs are going to pass other dogs. Now people, we don't need a dogfight, so use a little common sense here. Don't heel your pet right at another. There's about six feet between each of you, which should give us plenty of room. But remember: Your dog can glance at another as he goes by. That's normal. But if your dog takes so much as one step toward another dog, don't wait to see what he's going to do next. Yank your leash and go the other way. At the same time, say, "No! Fuss!"

Just worry about your own dog. Don't watch anything except him! Okay, ready? Go! Watch your dog!

After running the group through this exercise four to six times, we move on to the down-stay.

DOWN-STAY

Today we're going to teach these dogs to lie down. Let me show you how. May I borrow your Dalmatian a moment? Thanks. C'mon there, pup, let's move to where everyone can see what's going on.

Teaching "Platz!"

Sit! Good sit! Okay, the dog is sitting.

Then I kneel next to him.

Now watch.

After getting the dog onto the ground, I pet him while talking to the group.

Here's what happened. I said, "Sit!" and knelt next to Pooch. Don't kneel in front of him, that'd make him come to you before lying down and we don't want him to move before he lies down. I tapped the ground in front of the dog and said, "Platz!" That's "Platz!" Like lots only with a "p" in front of it. It's a German word that means "place," as in "Place yourself there!" Then I got the dog onto the ground the easiest way I could. Sometimes you'll sweep the front legs from under the animal while pushing on the shoulders. Some of the dogs are leaning against you; gently pull them downward in the direction they're leaning. You'll just have to experiment a bit and see what works best for your dog. Don't pull on the collar, though. That's like a correction and you don't correct a dog for things he doesn't know.

As the dog touches the ground tell him, "Stay!" Tomorrow, say, "Stay!" a little quieter. Quieter still the next day, and the word should be gone by the day after that. The idea is to build "Stay!" into the notion of "Platz!" so your dog will get on the ground and stay there. Right after you say, "Stay!" tell pooch, "Good platz!" After a few seconds, move him a little ways and do it again. Just say, "C'mon, pup," or something like that, when you move him; don't heel him. If you say, "Fuss!" between each "Platz!" the dog might think automatic sit is being replaced with automatic platz. Okay, try it. Get away from each other and teach "Platz!"

"No platz?" With this technique even large animals can be quickly taken to ground.

After the kids have worked on "Platz!" for a few minutes, I call them together.

You're doing well, guys. Tomorrow just bend next to the dog; don't kneel next to him. The day after that, get him to platz with you standing normally next to him. Any questions?

"My dog rolled onto his back. What should I do?"

"Nothing yet; he's trying to do the right thing. Settle for that for now, rather than tell him 'Not good enough!'"

TO MAKE LIFE EASIER

Here's a trick for working on "Platz!" Before you practice it each day, tire your dog with several minutes of fast heeling. If it's a warm, sunny day, heel in the sunshine and teach "Platz!" in the shade. Don't exhaust your pet, but heel just long enough and just fast enough so that the chance to lie down may look pretty good to him. When the animal is tuckered out from the heeling, show him "Platz!" three or four times quickly. After the last time, let him stay grounded for a few minutes while you sit next to him, telling him what fine work he's doing.

PLATZ CORRECTION

Once you're sure your pet has the idea—like after the first time he lies down without your help—the correction is stepping onto the leash or by yanking the lead downward, whichever is easier for you. Don't step or yank straight down; that could sprain a front leg. Step or yank toward yourself, at a slight angle.

How hard you correct depends on how tough your dog is. As with any first-time correction, it's better to start by undercorrecting than to scare with too much force. Remember, your next correction can always be tougher. Don't use the step-on-the-leash correction with a small dog; he might think you're going to step on him. With a small dog, it's better to pull the leash down with your hand instead.

Okay, work on "Platz!" for a few more minutes.

After everyone has had time to "Platz!" their pet three or four times, I call the group together.

One last thing: Practice "Platz!" separately. Don't use it while you're working on heeling, for instance. Make it a special lesson for now, to draw more attention to it.

Questions? No? You're doing well, people; so are your dogs. Stay with it. Here are this week's take-home sheets. Okay, then. I'll see you next week. Thanks for coming.

[NAME OF COMMUNITY] DOG TRAINING PROJECT

OBEDIENCE I WEEK 4

Training Exercise	Command	Per Session	Foundational or 7-Day Objective
1) Heel on Leash w/ Automatic Sit	FUSS	As Needed	Dog's attention w/ distractions
2) Sit-Stay	STAY	2 to 4	10' - 90 Seconds
3) Down-Stay	PLATZ/STAY	4 to 6	10' - 90 Seconds

DISTRACTIONS

Some good distractions are animals, playgrounds, people and noises. Unfair distractions are your dog's food dish, family members calling it, a stranger acting unfriendly or play toys.

DOWN-STAY

With pooch sitting at heel, command, "Platz!" and place him in the down position, saying, "Stay!" as he touches the ground and then praising, "Good platz!"

REFLECTION

Destiny is not a matter of chance,
it is a matter of choice; it is not a
thing to be waited for, it is a thing
to be achieved.

WILLIAM JENNINGS BRYAN

13

TRAINING SESSION FIVE

"PLATZ!"DOESN'T MEAN "ROLL OVER!"

Last week I told you not to do anything if your dog platzed onto his side or back. Pooch was trying to do his best. It would have been too soon to say, "That's not quite right." Now that they're at least going to ground when they should, let's help the dogs who aren't platzing straight better understand just what we want.

First, try this: Command, "Platz!" and as your pet lies down, rub his back. Most dogs like that and it can't be done, of course, if the animal rolls over.

Another deflective method is merely heeling your pet from the down position very quickly. It will soon see you won't wait for him to roll back over and hop up. He will learn it's to his advantage to platz in a straight, on-paws posture, to be ready to move out.

INTEGRATE

Also last week I told you to practice "Platz!" separate from other things your dog knows. Now you should start practicing it with those other things. I had you wait because it's better when teaching something new to hold off combining it with other things Pooch knows until he gets good at the new lesson. Dogs learn easier that way.

Returning in competition style after a stay.

SNIFF YE NOT!

Another problem connected to platz I see happening with a couple of dogs is they want to sniff the ground when they lie down. It's a natural reaction, but it can lead to creeping. I once watched a Doberman crawl at full sniff across an AKC ring to his handler during the down-stays.

Anyway, first command, "Platz!" As your dog hits the ground and starts to sniff, gently tug your leash sideways and say "No! Platz!" In other words, part of "Platz!" is "No sniffing!" If that causes Pooch to get up, block him with your hand across his withers—that's his shoulders, people.

Okay, work on "Platz!" for a bit.

THE STAYS

This week the sit-stay and the down-stay are at ten feet for a minute and a half. That's longer and farther than competition calls for, but you want to train a competition dog a bit farther than you have to. To maintain control, either get a longer leash or attach a line to your six-foot leash. If you use a thin line with a large or powerful dog, wear gloves to protect your hands against friction burns.

COMPETITION STAYS

In competition you must return from a stay by walking counterclockwise around your dog, stopping in the heel position. The first time you do it, Pooch may move when you go by. So watch for movement when you first try this return. If your pet moves, quickly stop him by putting your hands on him. Show your dog he must stay until you tell him to move. Now let's try it once—command, "Stay!" and leave your dog; count to ten and return, walking counterclockwise around him.

DISTRACTION

Last week we talked about distractions and we set one up during heeling. Let's create one related to sit-stay. Line your dogs up facing the center of the room, command, "Stay!" and head for the end of your leash. Now, while you guys are standing there looking at your dogs, a few parents I talked to earlier are going to walk back and forth five or six feet behind the animals. If this causes your dog to move, correct him back into position.

Okay, that's a minute. Return to your dogs and don't forget to walk clock-wise around them. Now praise your dogs. Let's try it again. Leave your dogs; the judge will say that to start a stay. Okay, parents, walk behind this lineup again.

After a minute I tell the group, "Return to your dogs," and we move on to the figure eight. As you can see, in addition to working the exercises, I'm getting the kids used to ring directions.

Distraction conditioning during a sit-stay.

FIGURE-EIGHT HEELING

People, there's a competition bit of heeling known as the figure eight. *Two parents are helping us, standing eight feet apart and facing each other. Now, let me borrow a dog for a minute or two. Could your Collie and I take a walk? Thanks. Okay, here's the starting position, a few feet back from a line between the parents, facing the gap between them and standing so that Pooch, not me, is centered between them. This is where you start. Now I'll pretend a judge just said, "Forward," and we'll heel in an eight-like pattern around the parents. Fuss!*

After showing the group the pattern, I return the dog and ask for questions. If there are none, I fill in a few blanks the kids may not have noticed.

Now, in the ring when you're doing the figure eight, the judge's directions—other than asking "Are you ready?"; they always ask that before any exercise—the directions will be "Forward" and "Halt" or "Stop." "Forward" means you tell your dog "Fuss!" and get moving, of course. "Halt" or "Stop" means just that: Quit walking.

When you're doing the Figure Eight and the judge tells you "Forward," always start to your left. That is, you have to start around one parent or the other—in the ring they're called posts, by the way—so make it the post to your left (unless the judge tells you to start around the other one, of course; always do what a judge tells you.) The reason for not starting to your right is that

Figure-eight heeling.

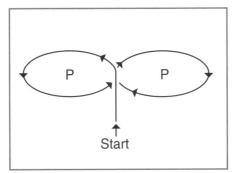

Figure-eight *heeling pattern (starting to the left; P stands for* Post).

Most dogs love to jump, but should one balk, he should be gently lifted over it so he can see it's safe.

direction has you going away from your dog, and it might cause a tight leash for a second. In competition, a tightly held leash is a cause of lost points. Practice starting either way, but in the ring go left.

I enlist the help of a few more parents as posts so students don't have to stand around while one team heels, and we work on the figure eight.

OVER JUMP AT HEEL

Guys, see this board I've set on its side here? It's a minijump. We're going to teach these dogs to jump over it as they heel with you. It's not a competition thing—we're doing it to make heeling more fun for your dog; most dogs like to jump.

To show your pet what you want, heel to the board and jump over it, saying, "Hup!" as you do. Don't just step over the board—jump over it. If you step over it, so will your dog; but if you jump over it, Pooch will imitate you.

Most dogs enjoy jumping, but if one is nervous about the board, lift him over it until he sees it's safe. Okay, line up here and, one at a time, heel over the jump. Praise, "Good hup!" just after Pooch goes over the board. After you jump your dog, go to the end of the line and get set to go again. Ready? Go!

CORRECT WORKING HEIGHT OF A JUMP

In setting up a jump at home, keep the height low for now. Raise it over a period of several weeks. How high? Don't make it higher than your dog's withers or higher than either of you can safely jump.

After several minutes of watching the class heel over the obstacle and listening to the sound of youthful laughter (and reflecting how lucky I am to be working with children and dogs), we end the session.

[NAME OF COMMUNITY] DOG TRAINING PROJECT

OBEDIENCE I WEEK 5

Training Exercise	Command	Per Session	Foundational or 7-Day Objective
1) Heel on Leash w/ Automatic Sit	FUSS	As Needed	Dog's attention w/ distractions
2) Sit-Stay	STAY	2 to 4	15'- 90 seconds
3) Down-Stay	PLATZ/STAY	4 to 6	15'- 90 seconds
4) Over Jump (at Heel)	HUP	4 to 12	Association w/ command "Hup!"

FIGURE-EIGHT HEELING

Practice this around Mom and Dad, lawn chairs and other "posts." Remember to start toward your left.

OVER JUMP AT HEEL

Keep the jump height low for now. Raise it gradually to your dog's proper working height. Don't make it higher than your dog's withers or higher than either of you can safely jump.

REFLECTION

There is no failure except in no longer trying.

ELBERT HUBBARD

TRAINING SESSION SIX

*Last week I told you the judge would say "Forward" and "Halt" or "Stop" during the Figure-Eight. In the ring you'll also do a holding pattern. The judge will tell you "Forward," "Right turn," "Left turn," "About turn," "Slow," "Fast," "Normal," and "Halt" or "Stop." A right turn is ninety degrees to the right and looks like this—*I demonstrate a right turn—*a left turn is ninety degrees to the left, like so—*I demonstrate a left turn—*and an about turn is 180 degrees, like this—*I demonstrate an about turn. *Notice you turn right for the about turn. Slow and Fast mean what you think they do: Walking slowly or running. Normal means walk at your normal speed. Any questions?*

Okay, let me run each of you through a heeling pattern, working you guys two at a time several feet apart. We'll be doing this a lot from now on, so be sure to practice at home.

After each student has had an opportunity to heel a pattern, we progress to the recall.

THE RECALL

WHAT IS IT?

The recall—"Come to me"—is like heeling because it allows a dog to be with his trainer. It's different because "Fuss!" has Pooch at your left side, while "Here!" teaches him to sit in front of and face you after coming to you.

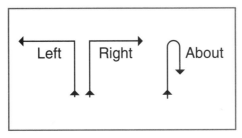

Left, right and about turns.

IT'S A LOCATION

"Fuss!" and "Here!" refer to positioning. "Fuss!" tells the dog to stay at a position next to you. "Here!" doesn't just order a dog to come to you, it tells him to sit in front of and face you. Whether he'll come should never be a question. If you take it for granted your dog will come when called, he probably will.

TEACHING METHOD

Let me borrow a dog for a minute. Guys, this is what's going to happen. I'll start with "Stay!" I'll leave the dog sitting, not in the platz. Because the recall teaches Pooch to come to you and sit, most dogs learn the pattern easier when called from a sit to a sit. Then I'll go to the end of the leash. I'll command, "Here!" and run backward. As the dog gets close to me, I'll stop and say, "Sit!" Then I'll praise, "Good here!" and pet him under the chin, so he will look up at me. Watch.

After calling dog to me, I tell the kids a bit more.

Notice the leash was slack during the lesson. There's no need to pull your dog to you. Your sudden movement draws him. Phase out "Sit!" over a few days as you did when teaching auto-sit at heel. As your dog catches on, lessen your running backward until you no longer need to do it.

COMMON SENSE

When your dog gets to you, you command, "Sit!"; but don't correct him if he sits slowly or crooked. A person doesn't call a dog and "reward" with punishment when the animal gets there. That just isn't done. A dog with any sense won't come again, certainly not happily. Clumsy your dog into the sit if you must, but don't correct him into it.

Okay, work on the recall for a little while.

After a few minutes we cover other recall aspects.

The recall. Note that the leash should remain slack while teaching this exercise.

NOT MORE THAN SIX FEET

Don't call from farther than six feet this week. With your running backward, your dog will cover more distance. Calling from farther away too soon can teach a dog to zigzag.

HOW STRAIGHT IS STRAIGHT?

If Pooch sits crooked, practice recalls along buildings or fences to the side where Pooch swings his butt, to block it and build the proper habit.

REMINDER

Don't use your dog's name with "Here!" Later the name can be an ace if it hasn't been used during training. Since competition allows using the name, if

Pooch looks away just as you're about to call him, you can get his attention back by saying his name just before, "Here!"

NOT YET

For now, don't use "Here!" to call your dog when he's off leash. If you do and if he doesn't come to you, he sees that he can ignore, "Here!"

After a recall, you go to the heel position; don't try to move your pet to heel. That would be too much to teach at once and could say he should go to heel automatically.

CONFUSION

When told, "Sit!" some dogs try to sit at heel, instead of in front of you. If it happens, don't assume your pal is being disobedient; it can mean you've got a pretty bright animal—he's trying to go where he thinks he should. Don't correct him for trying to do right—guide him to the "Here!" location—show him what "Here!" means.

Questions?

Let's work on recalls for a little longer, then we'll wind things up for this week.

One point about teaching the recall via my "running backward" technique: Know what is behind you! These photographs deliberately had the park bench behind me to make the point, but had I not known it was there, I could have wound up wearing this Rottweiler.

[NAME OF COMMUNITY] DOG TRAINING PROJECT

OBEDIENCE I WEEK 6

Training Exercise	Command	Per Session	Foundational or 7-Day Objective
1) Heel On-Leash w/ Automatic Sit	FUSS	As Needed	Dog's attention w/distractions
2) Sit-Stay	STAY	2 to 4	20' - 2 minutes
3) Down-Stay	PLATZ/ STAY	4 to 6	20' - 2 minutes
4) Over Jump (at Heel)	HUP	4 to 12	Association w/command "Hup"
5) Recall	HERE	4 to 8	6' from Sit

RECALL

Teach the recall by commanding, "Stay!" (sitting) and going to the end of your lead. Command, "Here!" and run backward. As your dog nears you, stop and command, "Sit!" Praise, "Good here! Sit!" as you pet your dog. Phase out "Sit!" as your companion catches on, as you did with the auto-sit at heel.

REFLECTION

Even if you're on the right track, you'll get run over if you just sit there.

WILL ROGERS

TRAINING SESSION SEVEN

STAND-STAY

TEACHING METHOD: SMALL DOGS

With smaller dogs the stand is most easily taught from the sit with a light, left-handed tap under the midsection as you command, "Wait!" I use "Wait!" because the "S" sound in stand *can cause a quick worker to sit.*

Once standing, pet the front and center of your dog's back. Pooch likes that and will push against the nice feeling, keeping himself standing. Command, "Stay!" and move away a step or two for a few seconds. Then return and praise, "Good stay!"

TEACHING METHOD: MEDIUM-SIZED TO LARGE DOGS

Larger dogs generally learn the stand more easily while moving at heel. A finger tap on the left flank when commanding, "Wait!" often freezes a dog in place. He might look left to see what touched him, but you can easily get his attention back by petting his head's right side. Don't pull the leash, though—that could make him sit.

Be sure to work with the outside flank, not the inside one. That is, with Pooch at heel, target the flank away from you. Touching the inside flank can cause your dog to spin away from you. He can't do

Teaching the stand to a smaller dog.

that when you touch him on the outside flank as your leg is in his way; it blocks the dog. Don't grab a flank. That can hurt the dog. The flank is very sensitive and you could get bitten.

After demonstrating the stand with a few dogs, I have the students work on the exercise for several minutes. Then I tell them some more about the stand.

PERSPECTIVE

The stand's objective isn't endurance. The sit-stay and the down-stay are practiced in minutes, the stand in seconds. Don't use this or any stay at the vet's office if the visit might be painful or unsettling. That's not obedience's purpose. Okay, work on it for a few more minutes.

Next we have the dogs hold a sit-stay while being petted by parents, conditioning that will lead to the stand-for-exam.*

People, let's practice the sit-stay. Line your dogs up facing the same direction, get them sitting, command, "Stay!" and go to the end of your leash.

---

*Parents should not approach their own children's dogs until the animals have had a couple of weeks' practice at being petted in a training framework.

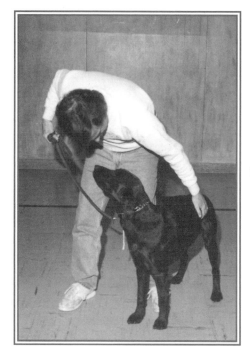

Teaching the stand to a larger dog.

Now, while you guys are standing there at leash's end, these parents I've asked to help us are going to go from dog to dog, gently pet the animal and walk away. If your dog moves from the sit, don't wait for me to tell you to go to Pooch and show him that just because someone pets him does not mean "Stay!" is canceled. Okay, parents, have at it.

After the last dog has been petted I tell the group, "Return to your dogs; remember to walk counterclockwise around them when you go back and to just stand next to your pet when you get there—don't praise your dog yet." Then, after a few seconds, I tell the kids, "Exercise completed—now praise your dogs."

New business: In competition you can't use a pinch collar, only a metal choker. Bring chokers next week and I'll show you how to change from one to the other.

[NAME OF COMMUNITY] DOG TRAINING PROJECT

OBEDIENCE I WEEK 7

Training Exercise	Command	Per Session	Foundational or 7-Day Objective
1) Heel On-Leash w/ Automatic Sit	FUSS	As Needed	Dog's attention w/distractions
2) Sit-Stay	STAY	2 to 4	20' - 2 minutes
3) Down-Stay	PLATZ/ STAY	4 to 6	20' - 3 minutes
4) Over Jump (at Heel)	HUP	4 to 12	Association w/command "Hup"
5) Recall	HERE	4 to 8	10' from Sit
6) Stand-Stay	WAIT/STAY	4 to 6	6' - 30 Seconds

STAND-STAY

With small dogs, teach the stand from the sit position by a light left-handed tap under Pooch as you say, "Wait!" Large dogs generally learn "Wait! more easily while moving at heel. A left-handed tap on the *left* flank can freeze a dog in his tracks. Then praise, "Good wait!" and pet the center of your pal's back.

REFLECTION

Losers visualize the penalties of failure. Winners visualize the rewards of success.

DR. ROB GILBERT

TRAINING SESSION EIGHT

THE FINISH

"People, do you know what an obedience finish is?"

"That's when we go home?"

Not quite. A dog finishes by moving from the recall's front-sit position to the heel position; from the "Here!" position to the "Fuss!" position.

TEACHING

To teach the finish, start with your dog sitting at heel. Hold your lead left-handed. Command, "Stay!" and step in front of and facing your pet from a few inches. You should be close enough to touch your dog; he should be where he would be if you'd called him. Command, "Fuss!" and quickly step backward and then forward with your left foot. Don't move your right foot. Your pet is used to following your leg movement when he hears "Fuss!" and moving your leg is to get him going without using force. Guide your dog past your left side and turn him toward the heel position. As he sits, praise, "Good fuss!" Phase out the leg movement as your companion catches on.

After demonstrating the finish with a few dogs, I turn the kids loose to teach their pets the exercise. Then I give them a bit more finish information.

A key to teaching the inside (or outside) finish is that the length of the handler's step backward must be sufficient to allow the dog room to turn and align at the handler's side. Note the difference in length of step called for by these two dogs.

OBEDIENCE: FIRST YEAR/ ON LEASH

Teaching the "outside" or "go-around" finish.

Another type of finish, the flip. Here Jackie, Roger Davidson's Springer Spaniel, jumps from the "Here!" position to the "Fuss!" position. Roger has been an instructor with the local 4-H dog program for many years.

If your dog consistently tries to go to your right and around you, let him. That's an acceptable pattern, too, just so he winds up in the heel position.

DON'T MISREAD PRIDE AS DISOBEDIENCE

Sometimes, when he first arrives at the heel position, a dog is so pleased with himself he forgets to sit. He may not even know he should. If your dog does this, don't correct him. Show him the finish and say, "Sit!" He'll catch on soon enough. Okay, work on the finish a little longer.

NOT YET

In competition the finish follows the recall, but practice the finish separately from the recall for now. Work on recalls for awhile, then work on the finish for a few minutes. If you do the two exercises together, a dog might think he should finish automatically.

CHOKE COLLARS

You're doing well, guys, real well. Bring your dogs over here and let me tell you about switching from a pinch collar to a choker. Remember last week I told you a pincher can't be used in the ring? Your dogs must wear chokers in an obedience trial? Here's how you make the switch.

Put the choke collar on but leave your leash attached to the pinch collar. Then, in a minute, you'll do some heeling, just to work Pooch while he's wearing both collars. Tomorrow, same thing: One dog, two collars. But tomorrow, after heeling for a short time, switch your leash to the choker. Then do a little more heeling. The next day, same thing—switch your leash to the other collar after a few minutes of heeling and heel some more. Then remove the pinch; put it in your pocket. Heel your dog. If you have to correct Pooch, put the pinch back on real fast and correct him with it. That's the key to this method, guys: Your dog doesn't know you won't yank the pincher out of your pocket and use it in the ring. You know you can't, but it doesn't. See?

Anyway, I've noticed most of you are really getting something going with your pets. You're bonding with them. The more you do that, the less they'll need correcting anyhow. Okay, chokers on and let's do some heeling.

We practice with chokers for awhile and end the session.

REFLECTION

When love and skill work together,
expect a masterpiece.

JOHN RUSKIN

[NAME OF COMMUNITY] DOG TRAINING PROJECT

OBEDIENCE I WEEK 8

Training Exercise	Command	Per Session	Foundational or 7-Day Objective
1) Heel On-Leash w/ Automatic Sit	FUSS	As Needed	Dog's attention w/distractions
2) Sit-Stay	STAY	2 to 4	20' - 2 minutes
3) Down-Stay	PLATZ/ STAY	4 to 6	20' - 3 minutes
4) Over Jump (at Heel)	HUP	4 to 12	Association w/command "Hup"
5) Recall	HERE	4 to 8	10' from Sit
6) Stand-Stay	WAIT/STAY	4 to 6	6' - 30 Seconds
7) Finish	FUSS	6 to 10	Understanding

FINISH

To teach the finish, start with your dog sitting at heel. Command, "Stay!" and step in front of and facing Pooch from a few inches away. Hold the leash in your left hand, say, "Fuss!" and step quickly backward and then forward **with your left foot**. Guide your dog to the heel (sit) position and praise, "Good fuss!" For now practice the recall and the finish separately.

TRAINING SESSIONS NINE, TEN AND BEYOND

Weekly meetings now consist of ring practice. The plan is to help students become accustomed to responding to ring directions and to the idea of being in the spotlight.

STAND FOR EXAMINATION

People, do you remember how you had your dogs hold a sit-stay while parents petted the animals? Let's do it again, only this time let's use the stand-stay. In the ring you'll do the stand individually; we'll do it here in group just to save time.

RECALL PRACTICE

Line your dogs up facing this way in a sit-stay. Now command, "Stay!" and go to the end of your leash. In the ring the judge will tell you, "Leave your dog," which you just did. Then the judge will tell you, "Call your dog." Okay, call them. Then the judge will tell you, "Finish."

ATTITUDE: RECALLS

An easy method for raising recall attitude is having several helpers form a corridor several feet apart, and recalling Pooch through the center while the assistants clap and cheer, "Good here! Good here!" They should begin applauding at the instant the dog moves in response to "Here!"

Heightening recall attitude through mass approval.

POINTS TO COVER DURING THE NEXT FEW WEEKS

Please read chapter 31, *"Rules and Procedures,"* and chapter 32, *"Before, During and After the Show."*

A MYTH, REVISITED

The first page of chapter 1, *"Focus on Students,"* examines the myth that children cannot train dogs as well as adults. I accent that fallacy in the following manner.

As you know, starting a couple of weeks after teaching heeling and the auto-sit, I have the group practice those exercises by having them heel along an area about forty feet square. Parents stand at each corner to outline the square. I stand in the center and start and stop the class, "Forward!" and "Halt!" As a dog does proper work—such as sitting automatically at heel—I pull the team out of the pattern and let the others keep at it.

A variation is as follows. When a dog misses an auto-sit, or does an extremely crooked sit, or is heeling two feet behind his trainer— in other words, when I see a major error relative to the length of training—I call that team into the center of the square with me. Pretty soon one handler and dog is left—that person wins the round.

It's an effective technique for several reasons. The sound and motion are good distractions for kids and dogs alike, and the youngsters get used to responding to a "judge's" directions and to "competing."

But what does this have to do with the training abilities of children versus those of adults? Just this: I invite selected students from my adult classes to work their animals at the kids' practices. They get to condition their dogs at a strange place and the youngsters get a chance at "beating" an adult. Usually several adults and their dogs are part of the heeling pattern, and seldom does an adult win a round. On the rare occasion when an adult does come in first, the kids are generally motivated to try harder. When a youngster is the last handler left, which is often the case, and he or she looks to the center of the square and sees adults that didn't make it, the child tends to grow a couple of inches.

SOMETHING TO THINK ABOUT

Let me tell you all something before we end this session. All of you are doing real well. So are your dogs. Each dog is trying—that's the important thing—and as long as your pet is trying to do right, be happy for that. Only one dog here can be Number One in the ring—that's how competition is—but each of these animals should always be Number One to you. Number One or Number Last means absolutely nothing in terms of what your dog feels for you, and that's what really counts.

REFLECTION

Do what you can, with what you
have, with where you are.

THEODORE ROOSEVELT

OBEDIENCE: NOVICE

CHAPTER 18

OFF-LEASH TRAINING

This section consists of a single chapter. That's because the only difference between Novice and First-Year and On-Leash routines is the absence of a leash—except for the down-stay being three minutes instead of one.

OVERVIEW

Most initial off-leash work is best presented to Pooch as something of a bluff.

Your pet has probably seen that you have powers and capabilities he can't understand. You can make a play toy fly over great distances; a movement of your hand lights up a room as you enter, darkens it as you leave. Your dog comes to accept such events without grasping how they occur. He will also learn you can contact him physically across wide distances, to govern his actions without appearing to be able to. That's what I mean about running a bluff.

The basis for this approach is it addresses real-world situations. Consider: If you are several hundred feet from your dog, there is no way he can be physically forced to do (or not do) anything, short of using a shock collar. The trick is not to let your pet discover this fact.

Rapport ultimately replaces mechanical and procedural techniques. Still, various training methods are necessary toward finalizing the process. A dog will always be a dog (thank God), and until the animal realizes you are totally in control, the human-canine relationship cannot develop to its fullest potential.

Now, before getting this chapter's lessons underway, we must examine a related matter.

CORRECTIONS

I bet we have something in common, you and I: Neither of us approves of mistreating dogs. Whether the specifics refer to poor care or out-

Practicing off-lead stays at a distance has a reinforcing effect on a dog's behavior. True, the handlers have no way of physically controlling their pets in this setting, but by working the animals thus, they sense that they are expected to remain, and dogs do what they are expected to do once they understand what those expectations are.

and-out abuse, we despise it. When discussed in terms of obedience, thoughts come to mind about abuse resulting from overcorrection. It's a wicked practice, one that's sadly all too common. Some methods promoted in training's name are disgusting.

A related yet less-acknowledged type of cruelty is undercorrection. Though to some it may seem a training kindness, in truth it's just another extreme, representing comparable mistreatment.

In theory, whether working on leash or off, corrections should be consistent in their degree of force, no more, no less. In practice, though, trainers can slip into the trap of nagging-type corrections. This usually occurs during the on-lead phase.

At heel the dog sits very slowly or extremely crookedly:

"Well, at least he sat."

It takes three progressively louder "Platz!" commands to get the dog onto the ground:

"Should I have corrected after my first command?"

Attention during heeling is everywhere but on the handler:

"Oh, well. No sense in getting after Pooch."

In all three instances, and others like them, lack of proper correction perpetuates the problem. It delays an inevitable confrontation, ultimately leading to more force than would have been originally needed.

The dog learns (is taught) to wait the trainer out; that he can "get away with it."

This tendency toward undercorrection chiefly arises in the situation where before obedience training, the dog was nearly uncontrollable. Undesirable behaviors decrease after a few lessons, and the owner is so pleased he or she doesn't follow through when force is called for. He compares current behavior with what it was, not with what it could be. He backs away from the level of pressure that has brought owner and dog this far, and what the dog's obedience might have been never comes to pass. Behavior may even backslide. Pooch comes to see reduced corrections as annoyances instead of as avoidable consequences.

Without a change in trainer attitude, the outcome is that punishment will always be part of the dog's life. Rarely will a day be free of pressure. Though it's true the corrections are never very firm, it's equally true they'll never stop. In a very real sense, the result is a dog serving a life sentence of abuse.

A person can get by with repeated, minor corrections with a perpetually on-leash dog. The dog's work will never be very sharp, but the lead's presence provides a continual means of control. But a similar approach to off-leash work cannot and will not produce reliability. For example, should a trainer be using a light line (a long, thin cord) in place of a leash, and should the trainer undercorrect so often that Pooch learns the line is just a long, thin leash, then all the trainer has done is swap equipment. Essentially, the dog is still on leash.

The rules that corrections must always be slightly tougher than the dog and consistently applied relative to undesirable behavior apply equally to on- and off-leash work. The difference is that, during off-leash work, they can't be repeated over and over. Once the animal is truly off leash, there's no physical way to control it. Praise and correction must have accomplished their purpose by then.

Should a trainer be tougher during off-leash work than a dog's capacity to absorb correction? No, of course not. That's never right. But if you've slid into the undercorrection trap, stay on lead awhile and match force with your pet's sensitivity before proceeding. Other-wise you'll be framing off-lead control atop a weak and shaky found-ation. Then the outcome isn't just predictable, it's inevitable: The training will come apart, most likely in a situation where obedience is really needed.

EQUIPMENT

BASIC OFF-LEASH TOOLS

Off-leash obedience is taught through much the same training mechanics as on lead. Praise and correction are still the keys. Other than the bluff concept, the main difference is the use of additional equipment.

THROW CHAIN

Owners are sometimes shocked when first hearing about the throw-chain technique.

"Let me get this straight: You actually throw a length of chain at your dog? At man's best friend?"

Answer: Yes, but be aware we're not discussing heavyweight material here but mere ounces of hanging-lamp chain. It is hurled at an off-leash dog should the animal depart despite the trainer's expressed wishes. The goal isn't to hurt or injure Pooch—far from it. It's to startle, and to make him wonder how you did that—touched him at a distance. I tell students:

Don't try for maximum velocity. Pain isn't our purpose here. We're after the "Gotcha!" effect. Besides, the harder the throw the more chance of missing, which could frustrate you and perhaps amuse the dog.

Throw the chain only if Pooch is turned away, so as not to risk striking an eye. Also, you must be able to read that your dog is about to break to be able to react in time to pitch the chain accurately at its hindquarters. Waiting until Pooch is in full stride will have him out of range before you can throw the chain. Speaking about a dog that runs away during heeling, the chain should strike the animal before it's taken three bounds.

Once your pet is back in line, don't retrieve the chain. Should he see you pick it up, he could reason (in his own way) what happened, which would greatly lessen the method's effectiveness. Carry several chains, later picking up used ones after taking your dog from the area.

COLLAR TAB

A collar tab is a few inches of venetian-blind cord or similar material looped through the collar's live ring (to which you normally attach your leash). A tab shouldn't be so long that the dog might catch a paw in the loop. With small dogs a loop need not be made—a single line of cord is sufficient.

A throw chain. Attaching a piece of brightly tinted yarn facilitates locating the chain in tall grass or snow.

Often the tab is used in concert with a throw chain. Let's say your off-leash dog takes off during heeling. You accurately throw the chain at his butt, verbal-bridging "No!" just as it strikes, and seconds later you collar-correct the animal via the tab, reminding him, "Fuss!" The throw chain stops him; the collar tab provides a quick handle for reestablishing control.

LIGHT LINE

A light line is a long, thin, lightweight cord with as light a snap as will hold the dog. I've used lengths varying from fifteen to a hundred feet. Material can range from fishing line to venetian-blind cord, depending on the animal's size and strength. A hand loop is neither necessary nor desirable. The line should be able to be dragged safely, without a loop that could catch on brush and the like. Caution: You may need gloves to avoid cuts and friction burns from the line. Use of this equipment follows.

LIGHT LEAD

A light lead is a six-foot leash much lighter in weight than the primary lead. If you've been using a leather leash, a show lead will do. If a show lead is your primary leash, fishing line is adequate. Light-lead methods follow.

APPLICATIONS AND TECHNIQUES

MULTIPLE LEASHING

Start a working session with on-leash heeling. Following an auto-sit, sneak a light leash onto your pet's collar, perhaps while you're praising

A collar tab.

him. Don't remove the main leash, though; you should wind up with two leashes on one dog. Keep Pooch unaware of the second lead's presence. While holding both leashes in one hand, heel a bit more. Stop, remove the primary lead and throw it a few feet in front of and slightly to your dog's left, radiating smug contempt for the object. "We don't need *that* any longer, do we, pup!" Conceal the second lead's excess right-handed behind your back. Command, "Fuss!" and step off. One of three situations will develop: Your pet will heel along with you, he will remain in place or he will toddle off in pursuit of other activities.

Should your pet accompany you as commanded, fine. Many dogs adapt to being off leash without argument, having gotten any debates out of their systems during on-lead work. Praise, "Good fuss!" and, after a few moments, walk to the primary leash. Make a show of fastening it, to accent that it's been missing. Leave the second leash connected, carrying both with either hand. Heel briefly, repeat the full remove-the-main-lead sequence once and end the day's work. Training now entails

Having discarded the primary leash, this young trainer is ready to see how well his pet does when the animal thinks he is off leash.

more of the foregoing over longer periods of time and in the face of ever-increasing distractions.

If your dog is like some I've known, once he senses he's free of restraint he will remain in place when commanded "Fuss!" or be gone for the tall timber, more often the latter. Should Pooch remain stationary, a leash correction timed with a second "Fuss!" is proper. Should he attempt to flee, it's time to clarify a few things.

Allowing for size and temperament, the correction must fit the crime. Remember, the nature of off-leash training is such that the day will come when you won't have a leash to fall back on. Should your pet figure out that all you've done is switch leads, then that's all you've done: Change leashes. The idea to convey is, "Don't push me, dog. Don't abuse my trust in you."

Just as your dog hits the end of the lead, tell him, "No!" As he turns in your direction, let the leash slip from your hands, dropping it so you can grab it in a blink should you need to. Keep your hands at your sides after you drop the lead, in an open-palms posture that shows you're holding air. This seeming lack of means won't be lost on the dog. Go to him, walking along the leash in case Pooch again tests your influence. Point out, "I said, "Fuss!" and heel to the primary lead. Assuming the animal doesn't push the issue further (most won't), make a show of attaching the main leash. Unfasten the second lead and leave it where it falls; get it later. Command, "Sit!" (to finish on a high note), praise, "Good sit!" and pet your companion to show you feel no anger. Then take him from the area; don't train further today.

The memory to leave the dog with is this: You removed the leash, he tried to take advantage and somehow the roof fell in. Something went very wrong at a time when he was certain you couldn't control him.

During the next session, work on any obedience *other than* off-leash training. Let today's lesson simmer awhile. Then repeat the double-leash sequence. Be aware your dog may pay more attention to what's going on than before, so be extra sneaky when attaching the second lead.

A few successful sessions don't prove reliability. If at some point your pet is going to flee, better it happen in a controlled setting. The purpose behind such technique is to create situations whereby if your pet is someday going to take off, you're in a position to say obedience must be absolute, despite an apparent presence or absence of a leash.

IT'S POINTLESS

Students sometimes tell me, "Last week I sneaked the leash off my dog for awhile and he heeled just fine."

Sure. That's because only one of you knew he was off-lead.

When advancing to multiple-leash techniques, make no secret that the primary leash has been removed. You want Pooch to know it's gone. Otherwise you can't predict how he will respond once the lead is truly off.

THE "RECALL" TRICK

A favorite method for establishing off-leash control relates to the recall. The technique should be done only once during a three- to four-week period; otherwise a dog could learn too much. Like the preceding multiple-leash lesson, a secondary idea is preventing Pooch from discovering the method's technique. The goal is still to leave him with the sense that even though he thought he wasn't under your domination, he was.

Before bringing your best friend to the training site, lay a twenty- to fifty-foot light line in a straight line across the area. Then get your dog and heel to one end of the line. After the auto-sit, while praising and petting, secretly attach line to collar. Remove the leash, make sure your pet sees you toss it aside, command, "Stay!" and go to the line's other end. Once there, drop your hat or some such so you've an obvious reason to bend over—dogs may be dumb animals in that they lack speech capability, but they're not stupid. As you retrieve the fallen article, secretly grip the line. Give a *light* tug and immediately call your pet, "Here!"

No, those last two instructions aren't backward. Normally you'd pull on the line *just after* giving the command (assuming the dog responded improperly). But today you'll seemingly make a technical error: pulling the line *just before* commanding, "Here!" The purpose isn't to effect a correction (hence, the stipulated "*light* tug")—it's to "touch" the dog when he thought you could not. The animal should feel the minor pressure an instant before or as he hears you call.

This lesson's emphasis isn't the recall exercise at all. It only looks that way. What's actually being said to your dog is *you can touch him at a distance.* As he arrives and sits, remove the line and drop it while praising and petting. Leave the line where it falls, instead of calling attention to it by gathering it up. Take pooch from the training area for some quiet time. Further work at this point could cloud the lesson.

"HOW'D YOU DO THAT?"

Off-lead control can be enhanced by even more subtle, less direct methods. Allow your dog to drag a light line while you are both playing ball. After a few minutes, call him to you, *not* as a formal recall but on the order of, "C'mere, pup." If he runs past or away from you, keep your hands at your sides as you step on the line. The idea isn't a forceful correction that brings Pooch to an abrupt, bone-jarring halt. It's to slowly stop him. When he turns and sees nothing in your hands, he will wonder for a month how you did it.

What we're after is the *spillover effect,* whereby the main idea of an event seeps into all areas of reliability. That's why it's best not to use the lesson in a formal training setting. You and Pooch were playing, he wasn't in a working frame of mind and suddenly your control kicked in. That's a powerful lesson, especially in its long-range meanings.

THE BLUFF CONCEPT, REVISITED

As suggested earlier, the preceding off-leash training procedures can have quite a carryover effect into other aspects of your friend's obedience. All phases of a dog's work often improve soon after starting off-lead work. The animal learns you can physically control him without appearing to be able to do so. What Pooch won't figure out is how. He may discover the light line, and that your power has something to do with it, but he has no way of knowing how long the cord is, or into what areas of his life it can reach. For all the animal knows, it may be of infinite length and unlimited potential. Eventually he accepts the condition without understanding the whys and the wherefores. To underscore this chapter's opening statement, that's what's meant about initial off-leash work being something of a bluff.

A subtle aspect of off-leash work is that by keeping your dog's attention you keep control of him. Note that the contact between human and dog during some long-leash work is solid and constant.

CURVEBALL

Another off-leash training "technique" is throwing the play toy and, once your pal has grabbed it and is returning, step backward (to increase attraction) and say, "C'mere, pup." Sure, it was his idea to return, but make the dog think it was yours. Later, all the dog will remember is hearing your call while coming to you. This is subtle but a habit-builder nonetheless.

DEALING WITH THE POTENTIAL RUNNER

If you sense your dog may take off once you've dropped your lead during a stay, it's better to deal with the problem now than later. Command, "Sit!" or "Platz!" and then, "Stay!" Using a fifteen-foot leash, retain your hold of the looped end while dropping the excess in front of Pooch, but without him seeing you're still holding the lead. This can often cause a devious dog to think the leash has been abandoned entirely; that he's free to flee.

A subtle aspect of off-leash work is that by keeping your dog's attention you keep control of him. Note that the contact between human and dog during some long-leash work is solid and constant

Should the dog run, don't say anything, not a word. You have already said, "Stay!" Should your pet choose to ignore your command, give no further warnings about consequences. Merely brace yourself and allow the laws of physics to prevail. After he hits the end of the lead, bring the dog back to where you'd left him, apply a sit or platz correction (depending on which position you'd commanded) and depart again, with a somewhat bored-looking, shaking-of-the-head, disgusted air, one that says you've seen it all before (even if you haven't).

Should you be working with a giant that you feel could yank you out of your sneakers, modify the procedure by correcting the dog after he takes one step. Move to the side and tug the lead at a right angle to the direction of your dog's intended path. Accompany the correction with a memorable speech, one that begins with, "Now look!"

A QUICK HITTER

Another off-leash reinforcer can occur in and around the house. For example, you encounter your dog and say in passing, "Howdy, pup—Sit!" Praise the animal if he complies; immediately cause him to sit if he doesn't. (Pressure can be applied by using your hands like a pinch collar—grabbing neck hair and skin and pulling upward and toward yourself, similar in effect to how you taught the on-leash sit. Don't dig in with your nails—use your fingertips. The idea is to control, not to scare or injure.) Praise the dog as he obeys. Bring the dog out of the sit by petting him, commenting, "You're sure a neat dog," and perhaps getting him to walk with you a few paces. Then go about your business.

The entire "training session" lasted only seconds, but much was accomplished. Obedience was activated in a blink and *no collar was*

Let Pooch think you've dropped the leash. See what happens. If he stays with you, gather the leash up and tell your friend what a good dog he is.

required for control. Only your presence was needed. The nature of such subtle training builds lifelong habits.

CLARIFICATION

If all this strikes you as "training by confusion," you're right. If such technique seems flawed by definition, or immoral, unethical or less than forthright, you're missing the point.

That a confused dog shouldn't be corrected is stated in all my training books. But if you command your off-leash pet, "Fuss!" and he responds by taking off, the animal is hardly confused—he knows exactly what he's doing! He figured you had no physical control of him and decided to take advantage of it. That's a calculating canine, not a confused one.

As such behavior is intolerable, your response must say, "It's in your best interests not to try that again." You can't outrun Pooch, you lack his ability for quick starts and sudden turns, but when it comes to being downright sneaky, he's met his match: You can surely outthink him. As stated in chapter 7, "*Obedience Training Guidelines*," be one inch tougher than the dog, no more, no less. Toughness relative to *Canis familiaris* is not limited to physical force—mental toughness is part of the equation, too.

NOTE TO INSTRUCTORS

I don't provide weekly lesson written material beyond the First-Year and On-Leash level. My feeling is that by the time kids hit Novice, they should be learning to rely on their memories and their understanding of dogs and training.

REFLECTION

Aim for success, not perfection. Never give up your right to be wrong, because then you will lose the ability to learn new things and move forward with your life.

DR. DAVID M. BURNS

OBEDIENCE: GRADUATE NOVICE

CHAPTER 19

DROP ON RECALL

COMPETITION CONSIDERATIONS

In this exercise you interrupt the recall by commanding, "Platz!" when Pooch has come about halfway. Summon him a second time and end the exercise with a routine obedience finish.

Don't teach the drop before you've completed Novice competition. Novice requires an uninterrupted recall, and a dog that's been taught the drop could react incorrectly (*e.g.*, lie down while coming to you) when in the stressful environment of an obedience trial.

DOWN AT A DISTANCE

The drop on recall is taught through a series of steps. The first is to teach your companion to hit the ground from a stationary position at a distance from you.

Leave your dog in a sit-stay and move to a point two or three feet in front of and facing him. Keep the leash in your left hand, with enough slack that the lead hangs just short of the ground. As a quickly flowing sequence, raise your right palm—faced toward your dog—just above the level of your head. This is the platz signal. Hold it there for a second, verbally command, "Platz!" and step with either foot onto the leash, letting the signaling hand fall to your side.

Generate adequate foot power to down your pet quickly but make it suggestive, guiding pressure; don't strike the leash with the same force you'd use in a refusal-to-comply correction—toe-tap the lead. Praise, "Good platz," once the animal is grounded. After a few seconds, move him with, "C'mon, pup," or a similar verbal cue (don't say, "Fuss!"—we aren't working on heeling just now), and hurriedly repeat the exercise. Practice the sequence six times, then close the day's training.

When employing this guiding-foot-on-the-leash technique, move your foot no more than necessary when pinning the leash, so pooch

Teaching the down at a distance.

isn't taught a foot signal. Increase your signaling distance by a few steps daily, until your dog is correctly responding at thirty feet. Then use the same method to teach "Platz!" from the stand.*

DOWN FROM MOTION

The preceding work teaches your dog to hit the ground when commanded at a distance from you. Now we need to show the animal to platz while in motion.

---

*To adapt this work to the Utility Dog routine described in chapter 26, *"Hand Signals,"* once your dog has the idea, begin to soften and ultimately phase out "Platz!"

Timing is more important than sheer force when teaching the down from motion.

Dropping your leash in front of Pooch as you command, "Platz!" can be effective in showing him to hit the ground immediately—many dogs won't step on or over their own lead.

Warm up your dog with some quick and lively heeling. After an automatic sit, command, "Platz!" Take the animal down quickly should it respond sluggishly, reminding it platz must be fast.

Again command, "Fuss!" and establish a brisk pace. Carry the leash right-handed, with enough slack that it hangs just short of the ground. After a few steps, command, "Platz!" as your *right* foot touches the ground; then bring your *left* foot onto the lead. That's how long Pooch has to respond: the time it takes for your left foot to come forward and pin the lead.

As with the down-at-a-distance work, make your initial foot-on-the-leash pressure suggestive rather than corrective. For most dogs a toe-tap should be adequate force. Of course, if your companion downs promptly it'll feel no force because the leash, like the dog, is on the ground. As the animal platzes, praise, "Good platz!" and remind, "Stay!"

Thwarting the creeper.

Try to keep moving during this entire sequence; don't stop unless you have to. After moving away a short distance, return, heel your companion a few steps into an auto-sit and repeat the platz-while-heeling drill three times. End the session after the last run-through so as not to distract from the lesson with other activities. What remains is gradually lengthening the distance you cover after "Platz!" (the goal is thirty feet) and fading out "Stay!"

DROP ON RECALL: TEACHING

Increase to thirty feet the distance at which your dog reliably platzes from the stand-stay. Then commence the following on a surface that provides some friction, not one on which a dog could easily slide when stopping from a run.

Do a long, uninterrupted recall. A distance of thirty feet is adequate. "Stay!" Pooch after he arrives and sits, and depart again, going another thirty feet. Command, "Here!" As the animal nears the halfway point, walk quickly toward him while commanding, "Platz!" both verbally and with the hand signal. Repeat the commands as needed. Stop in place the instant your pet grounds, enthusiastically praise, "Good platz!" and call, "Here!" communicating a "What fun!" message. Quickly repeat the entire sequence once, then end the session. What remains is adjusting the pattern, remaining in place as you command, "Platz!" and delaying your second "Here!" for several seconds.

DOWN ON RECALL: ATTITUDE

A negative aspect of the drop is it can teach a slow recall. Forever a behaviorally patterned animal, a dog can learn there's no need to rush to the handler because he will shortly be directed to lie down. One way to maintain a high-flying attitude is to eliminate the down on recall for several weeks once Pooch has mastered it. He won't forget the lesson. Remember: Dogs learn for life. Then occasionally command the drop, communicating much excitement as you call your dog the second time.

THE CREEPER

There's a direct and convincing correction for the dog that persists in taking extra steps after being commanded to lie down. With a larger animal, go to him and lift him off the ground by encircling his neck (near the chest) with one arm and the area just behind its ribcage with the other. Don't grab the coat; your hands should clutch only air. Then vise-lock the dog with your arms. Carry him to the spot where he should have downed, transporting him so that he's looking backward. Emphatically place him on the ground (*place*, not *slam*); comment, "I said, Platz!" while pointing at the location; return to your starting point and continue the lesson. The technique is the same with a smaller dog, except the animal is lifted using your hands along his ribs. The effectiveness of this method lies in the fact that your dog hates being off-balance. He equally dislikes being carried so that he can't see where he's going. More than once I've seen a single application of this correction break creeping habits of several months' duration.

REFLECTION

Learn the art of patience. Apply discipline to your thoughts when they become anxious over the outcome of a goal. Impatience breeds anxiety, fear, discouragement and failure. Patience creates confidence, decisiveness and a rational outlook, which eventually leads to success.

BRIAN ADAMS

CHAPTER

20 RECALL OVER HIGH JUMP

In the ring this exercise is essentially a straight-line recall over a high jump. The routine heightens recall animation and enjoyment while teaching your dog to come to you over an obstacle. It's not only foundational for high-jump retrieving and directed jumping, it has the side effect of speeding up normal recalls.

TEACHING*

Set the high jump at one-third of your pet's height at the withers. If you're working Pooch on concrete or a similar surface, use ring floor mats or tape a section of carpet to the floor to make the take-off and landing areas safer. Heel over the jump twice, commanding, "Hup!" to

When teaching the recall over high jump to a smaller dog, you may want to skip striking the jump with your hand. The posture created by having to bend so far can seem intimidating to a smaller animal.

*It is assumed Pooch knows "Hup!" from being taught over jump at heel; see chapter 13, *"Training Session Five."*

Success!

put the dog's mind into jumping mode. Then leave pooch in a sit-stay three feet from and facing the jump. Step across the hurdle (to suggest the correct path) and face your dog, standing two feet from the jump. Slap the top board, command, "Hup!" and quickly move backward to attract your jumper and provide landing room. If sound bothers your dog, whack the board lightly. If noises excite him, hit the board a good lick.

Command, "Sit!" as your pal arrives, but don't be concerned if his response is less than perfect. Work on that only after he's doing well with jumping. Gradually raise the jump height as your dog gains confidence, but no higher than his withers.

THE END-AROUND PLAY

Should a dog come around the jump instead of over it, deflect rather than use force. Force can cause stress and stress inhibits jumping: A nervous dog hesitates to leave the safety of the ground. Place the end Pooch comes around against a building, fence or similar structure, making the end-run impossible. Should your pet react by trying to go around the other end, block that end with lawn furniture or by whatever means you have.

USE OF FORCE

Rarely is it necessary to pressure a dog over a jump. If force is needed, gently lift Pooch over the obstacle, praising, "Good hup!" as he lands.

Preventing a dog from coming around a jump.

 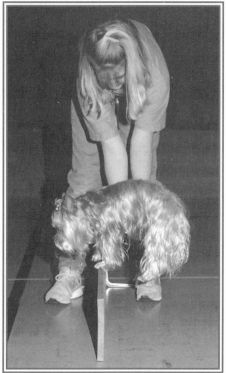

Use of "force" with a reluctant dog.

Then immediately command, "Sit! Stay!" and step across the jump and call him again. Once momentum is established, don't stop until the dog has had several successes.

REFLECTION

One can never consent to creep when one feels an impulse to soar.

HELEN KELLER

DIRECTED JUMPING

RECALL OVER BAR JUMP

Begin teaching this work once your dog is comfortable with the recall over high jump.

"Wait a minute! The Graduate Novice routine doesn't include the bar jump. Why are we teaching it now?"

"So we can then teach directed jumping."

"But Grad Novice doesn't require directed jumping either."

"I know. I also know Graduate dogs seldom come around the high jump during practice, but that they might in the ring in response to competition stress. Teaching directed jumping is a proofing method intended to direct the dog's mind away from "Will I jump?" and toward the concept of "Which jump?""

TEACHING

This work is not very different from the recall over high jump, except for the bar jump's appearance. Starting at low height, angle the bar across the high jump's top board. Practice recalls over this modified jump for four days, starting Pooch six to ten feet from the hurdle for this and following stages.

The next step is removing the bottom board, replacing it with lengths of doweling on each side equal to the width of the removed board (see figure on page 151). This maintains the current working height while creating a visible bottom gap.

A few days later, remove the next board from the bottom, replacing it with doweling equal in length to the combined width of the removed boards. If the dog tries to go under the obstacle, block and shove him back under the jump, then call or lift him over it.

Step one in teaching the recall over bar jump.

Step two is to remove the bottom board.

The finished product—recall over bar jump.

The final step is using the bar jump itself, eliminating the boards. Start with bar height equal to the middle of your dog's chest. Raise the bar gradually over a period of weeks until it's at the dog's correct working elevation. Call Pooch from the direction that, if he bumps the bar, it will fall away from the supports without toppling the entire structure, which could injure and frighten.

DIRECTED JUMPING

With your dog present, erect both jumps, configuring them at low height and setting them ten feet apart (see figure on page 153). Recall your companion over the standard high jump. Do it again.

Then walk your dog to a point *between* the obstacles and a dozen feet behind a line between them. Aim Pooch toward the high jump and command, "Stay!" Walk to a central spot relative to the obstacles and the dog (see figure on page 153). Emphatically point and step toward the high jump and command, "Hup!"

As Pooch sails over the correct jump, praise, "Good hup!" and take him back to the starting point. Command, "Stay!" and return to the

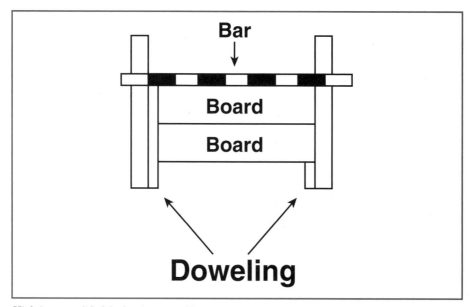

High jump modified for bar jump teaching.

Displayed above is my form of force for the dog that insists on going under the bar rather than over it.

location opposite your dog's, and repeat the exercise. Do the routine twice more, then end the session.

On the next day, repeat the preceding exercise once. Then "Stay!" your companion, having first aimed him toward the *other* obstacle, the bar jump. Return to your command location and—adding pronounced body language, such as pointing and even stepping toward the bar jump—command it over the bar jump. If he does as well with it as he did with the high jump (and he probably will), great! Rapport has saved you both a good deal of time and effort. Now the work becomes gradually raising the jump's heights, positioning them until they're twenty feet apart, phasing out aiming Pooch toward either jump, and starting him from at least twenty feet.

During the teaching sequence, should your pet take any action other than the correct one, don't scold him. It's likely you're taking him too far too fast. Back up a couple of teaching steps and stay at that level until he's ready to progress.

OBEDIENCE: GRADUATE NOVICE

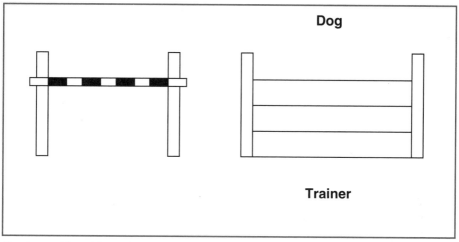

Starting position of dog and trainer.

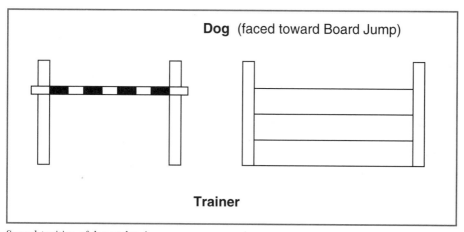

Second position of dog and trainer.

Don't go around saying the world owes you a living; the world owes you nothing; it was here first.

MARK TWAIN

The hand signal indicating the jump to be taken.

CHAPTER 22 OUT-OF-SIGHT STAYS

TEACHING TECHNIQUE

Out-of-sight stays are just what you think they are: The dog maintains a commanded position regardless of the fact that the trainer disappears from view. Obviously, such stays are eminently practical in addition to being competition elements. In Graduate Novice, handlers depart the ring in a group for the required times of one minute for the sit-stay and three minutes for the down-stay. In Open competition these times are three minutes and five minutes.

The out-of-sights are taught more easily by disappearing immediately, as opposed to walking a long distance before vanishing. The dog whose handler disappears quickly feels more secure than if the person fades at a long distance. Select a hiding place where you won't throw shadows and where the wind direction won't carry your scent to your pet. Lower confusion potential by using both voice and signal for "Stay!"

Build to the required times gradually, as you did when you first taught "Stay!" Also, overtrain. Graduate Novice times are the same as in Novice—one minute for sit, three for the down; train to two minutes sitting and five minutes lying down.

INSECURITY IS NOT DISOBEDIENCE

With a dog that has been stay-steady but that breaks during out-of-sights, insecurity is more likely the cause than disobedience. If your pet seems nervous about this modified stay, skip it for now; teach it when he becomes more secure.

Initial teaching of an out-of-sight sit-stay.

COPS CALL THEM SNITCHES

Teaching out-of-sights is easier with the help of a "fink" whose job is secretly cuing you should Pooch move. Communication must be subtle: A cough or dropping a hat will work nicely.

Use different helpers and change cues at least daily, lest the dog see and hear too much. More than once I've seen a dog holding a sit-stay lie down after the trainer disappeared; Pooch heard the helper's hiccup (or whatever) and hopped back into the sit before the trainer could return. Obviously, a dog can learn that a second person's sound or gesture means the trainer is returning. As I mentioned in an earlier chapter, dogs are accurately defined as dumb animals as they lack speech capabilities, but don't think that they're stupid. They aren't.

REFLECTION

It is common sense to take a method and try it. If it fails, admit it frankly and try another. But above all, try something.

FRANKLIN D. ROOSEVELT

OBEDIENCE: OPEN

23 RETRIEVING ON THE FLAT

In AKC-style competition retrieving, a handler commands the sitting-at-heel dog, "Stay!" and throws a dumbbell a short distance forward. On the judge's cue, the handler commands his or her dog to retrieve the article. The dog obliges, returns with the object and sits in front of the handler in recall fashion. The handler takes the dumbbell and commands the dog to finish.

ATTITUDE: YOUR PET'S

Because dogs are motivated by competition and imitation, stimulating these urges can not only save training time and effort, it can build attitude. For example, a tactic is working seasoned retrievers while inexperienced dogs watch (it's also good distraction conditioning for the performers).

Another attitude enhancer is having your dog carry an article (a play toy or a dumbbell) to another person, preferably a family member. Use a closed room to prevent wandering. With you and your helper sitting or kneeling several feet apart, hand your pet an object. As he mouths it, encourage him through voice and gesture to, "Take it Jerry," with Jerry being your assistant. At the same moment, Jerry should begin encouraging the dog to bring the article, praising him as he does so. When the dog arrives, Jerry should take the object, briefly examine it approvingly, then return it to your pet while encouraging him to carry it back to you, saying, "Take it (your name)," and pointing toward you. This intensifies retrieving interest while building attitude—the dog learns that carrying an object to a person is enjoyable.

ATTITUDE: YOURS

Many training systems seem based on the notion that teaching retrieving is a battle. They spend more time illustrating force methods than acknowledging that dogs are born with an instinct for retrieving. The result can be a self-fulfilling prophecy—harsh teaching styles have taught more than one sound retrieving prospect to fear a dumbbell and distrust the handler. Trainers can use force if needed, but unless Pooch resists, don't risk lost animation and rapport by presuming he'll contest the lessons. To do otherwise is to approach the project with a negative mind-set which risks sending a similar attitude down the leash.

SUBTLE FORCE

Be aware that force exists in my retrieving program from day one, though in subtle form. Pooch wears a pinch collar during all teaching situations; the sensation reminds him the trainer's words aren't to be taken lightly. As you see, effective force is not necessarily active; it can operate through warning as well as through action.

EQUIPMENT

The dumbbell should be a bit large and heavy to inspire a working attitude. Too small or light an object can cause a less-than-serious mind-set. Use a dumbbell that meets organizational requirements, but avoid missized articles relative to the dog.

REQUISITE

Teaching the retrieve on flat ground requires successful completion of Novice training. My approach to retrieving calls for extending patterns your pet learned during basic obedience. The retrieve develops from work the dog already knows; it's not presented as a new and distinct lesson.

Using too big a dumbbell can cause an otherwise willing dog to hesitate.

Inserting a finger behind a canine tooth can cause a dog to open his mouth.

TEACHING THE FLAT RETRIEVE: PHASE ONE

Begin the first session with a few minutes of lively heeling followed by a sit-stay. The purpose is to loosen up your dog, to put him in a working frame of mind. Then set your pet up for a second sit-stay. This time, though, before "Stay!" and stepping away, say, "Take it!" while making Pooch accept and hold a dumbbell. Should mild force be required, reach across the top of the muzzle and exert upward finger pressure behind the canine tooth (longest upper—be careful not to get nipped). This causes nearly any dog to open his mouth.

Command, "Stay!" and leave, going no farther and for no longer than when you first taught the sit-stay—a foot or so for five seconds. Return, take the dumbbell and praise, "Good stay!" If Pooch continues to hold on when you try to take the dumbbell, *don't* correct him. If he's that interested in keeping the object, so much the better. To cause the release, *gently* lift one end of the dumbbell, causing it to rotate in a manner (if not at a speed) like an airplane propeller. He'll let go.

The key to the first retrieving lesson is this: If your pet drops the dumbbell, or even starts to, make him see that's the same as a broken stay. We're linking the hold of a dumbbell with the concept of stay. Most dogs get the idea quickly, as letting go is a form of movement and

The first step in teaching the retrieve is sit-stay while holding a dumbbell.

Pooch already knows "Stay!" means "Don't move." Now you must teach the command also means "Don't let go." If your dog loosens his bite once you've said, "Stay!" instantly apply the verbal-bridge technique by saying, "No!" and replacing the article in its mouth.* The idea that a premature release is like a broken stay must be made abundantly clear. It may even be necessary at first to force the hold by gently grasping your pet's muzzle.

Practice the lesson four times a session. The goal isn't endurance—a dog should never be made to hold an object for more than fifteen seconds. When he will hold it for as long as it takes for you to walk a dozen paces away, count to ten and return, a level you should reach within a week, start the next stage.

TEACHING THE FLAT RETRIEVE: PHASE TWO

The next step is recalling your companion as it holds the dumbbell. Again, we're linking retrieving with work your dog already knows, in this case the recall.

*See chapter 12, *"Training Session Three."*

Step two in teaching the retrieve is adding the recall.

Start by using recall-teaching technique—calling over short distances as you move backward. Use "Here!" during the first few days. Your dog understands that command, while the retrieve command "Bring!" means nothing to him yet. When he's doing well with this modified recall, begin to increase distance and decrease back-pedaling.

Once your dog reliably recalls with the dumbbell from fifteen feet, begin commanding, "Bring!"—pause a second and take a step backward—"Here!" Once he's responding to "Bring!" you can start eliminating "Here!" by softening your voice until the word disappears.

ENVIRONMENTAL INFLUENCES

As you increase "Bring!" distance, start working in areas that cause your dog to retrieve slightly uphill. Steep inclines serve no purpose, but a slight uphill run causes your pet to work harder, leading him to concentrate more on business. When Pooch will "Bring!" the dumbbell from thirty feet, go to the next step.

TEACHING THE FLAT RETRIEVE: PHASE THREE

Conduct the following on flat ground, not on an incline.

Begin the day's session with a single, thirty-foot "Bring!" Then leave your dog on sit-stay, taking the dumbbell with you. Set the object on the ground two paces from your dog while glancing pointedly from the dog to the dumbbell. Back away two more steps while facing your pet. You should be facing your dog from four paces with the dumbbell halfway between you. Point at the object and command, "Bring!" One of seven things will happen.

1. The dog will pick up the dumbbell and bring it to you.

2. The dog will grab it and attempt to run away.

3. The dog will recall normally, without the dumbbell.

4. The dog will hold the stay.

5. The dog will depart, leaving the dumbbell behind.

6. The dog will stand and remain in place.

7. The dog will lie down.

HOW TO RESPOND

If the dog brings the dumbbell, which usually happens, praise, "Good bring!" as he arrives. Let your student know what a good job he did as you end today's session, to guarantee leaving him with a sense of accomplishment that any later "lesser than" performance could override. Don't worry about front-sit straightness and such—premature tinkering with such niceties can lessen confidence. Share your pleasure at your pal's understanding, fine-tuning the routine later. Continue this pattern for the next three days, increasing the dumbbell's distance from you and your pet by two feet daily and the number of retrieves by one.

Should the dog attempt to take off with the article, immediately say, "No!" and encourage "Bring!" Moving backward as you call Pooch may be all it takes to draw him to you. He's close to doing the right thing, his only mistake being direction. His sudden flight may be no more than a doggy version of keep-away or "Let's play!" It's wiser to modify a happy attitude rather than risk dampening it by force.

If your pet comes to you without picking up the object, don't respond with force unless you're certain he's resisting. That would be a rare case, indeed—seldom will a defiant dog come to the trainer during a disobedient act. More likely he's mixed up and is trying to do what he thinks is right. He has partially learned to associate "Bring!" with coming to you. Doing so without the dumbbell could easily be the sign of a dog that is trying to obey. It may be the dog thinks that since

Step three in teaching the retrieve is requiring the dog to pick up the dumbbell.

you didn't give him the object when you left, he isn't supposed to go near it. Lead Pooch to the article and suggest through word and gesture that he should pick it up. If he still seems confused, press his head down to the dumbbell and insert a finger behind a canine tooth to open his mouth. Remove your finger and—as his jaws close on the dumbbell—say, "Bring!" and back away encouragingly.

Should your pet continue to stay, he's probably confused. Repeat, "Bring!" while pointing at the dumbbell to move him from the stay into the desired response. Or pick up the dumbbell and back away while teasing the animal with it, encouraging him from a short distance to grab the object. Gradually lower the article until he's taking it very near—and then on—the ground.

The animal that runs off isn't ready for this pick-it-up phase. He needs more stay and recall practice while holding a dumbbell.

The dog that stands and remains in place is confused, not disobedient. Standing in this situation is asking for direction. Repeat, "Bring!" accompanied with gestures and body language to communicate your wish.

Similar is the dog that hits the ground. He's obviously confused and should be given encouragement, *not* disapproval or force. This dog has probably been brought too far too fast. Return to recalls while carrying a dumbbell for a few days.

"YOU PUT IT THERE—YOU PICK IT UP!"

If the dog refuses to grab the dumbbell—that is, Pooch knows what you want and defies you—you're faced with out-and-out disobedience that should be met head-on. I'm not talking about the animal that asks, "Say what?" or even the dog whose attitude is, "I'd really rather not." The first is unclear about the trainer's intent and the second can often be brought around by repeating the finger-behind-a-canine-tooth technique. I'm speaking about the animal whose message isn't just "No!" but "Absolutely not!" Given the work that's gone before, it's a rare creature that reacts like this, but if you're absolutely certain it's your dog we're discussing, proceed as follows.

Grasp the pinch collar's top chain left-handed and turn your fist clockwise to create pressure. Maintain the correction as you lead Pooch to the dumbbell, taking care the pressure doesn't stimulate your dog to bite, which can happen. As you arrive at the dumbbell, push the dog's head toward it while still twisting the chain. The instant that Pooch touches the object, stop the pressure and attract the animal by moving backward while encouraging "Bring!"

NOT YET

For now, do *not* formally command your friend to release the dumbbell. A better approach is praise for bringing it, followed by a mock tug-of-war. Bend or kneel in front of your pet, grasp the ends of the dumbbell and act as though you're having great difficulty taking it from him, complete with grunts, groans and gasps of effort. Don't worry if excitement draws the dog from the sit position as he struggles to hang on. The ideal result would be for your pet to wrench the object from you and bound away with his prize. When you need to reclaim the article to end the session, gently rotating the dumbbell by lifting either end will cause his release. Don't correct your friend should he still try to hold on—we don't want to teach a losing attitude. Just continue rotating the object until you've wrestled it away.

TEACHING THE FLAT RETRIEVE: FINAL PHASE

When your dog will reliably "Bring!" the dumbbell placed between you, take the final step. Put him in a retrieving mind-set by having him "Bring!" it once, using the pick-it-up-along-the-way method. Then, with Pooch at heel, command, "Stay!" toss the dumbbell three or four feet and command, "Bring!" If you sense uncertainty, walk your companion to the object and encouragingly clarify your wish. Should his attitude say, "You threw the thing—you go get it!" correct as you would for refusal during the pick-it-up-along-the-way lesson.

AFTER TEACHING THE RETRIEVE ON FLAT GROUND

A MINOR MATTER

Should your pet grab the dumbbell not by the crossbar but by an end, don't worry about it for now. Once it's solidly retrieving, work on the problem by repeatedly positioning the dumbbell correctly in his mouth. He will get the idea. Don't scold as Pooch picks up the dumbbell incorrectly—such timing could confuse: "What? Aren't I supposed to grab the dumbbell when you say 'Bring!'?" Let him take a few steps with the object before adjusting it.

Darryl Dockstader and his Alaskan Malamute, Nick, who seems determined to keep the dumbbell.

Correct this problem through patience, not force.

OUT!

Teach "Out!" ("Release!") by commanding, "Out!" and then gently rotating the dumbbell by lifting either end. A fingertip tap under the chin is another way of suggesting the release. A determined animal can be taught "Out!" through steadily increasing pinch-collar pressure (pulling the leash, rather than yanking it). Don't apply so much force that enthusiasm is dampened.

"OUT!" IS A SPOKEN COMMAND, NOT A SIGNAL

Teach Pooch that your act of reaching for the dumbbell does not mean "Out!" Otherwise you risk his dropping the article before you can take it. Instill a hang-onto-it attitude by encouraging tug-of-war with the object. Another technique is letting your pet walk among other (friendly) dogs while holding his prize. He probably won't drop it as he knows another could pick it up (this is another example of competitive training). Thoroughly condition by reaching for the dumbbell, gently tapping both ends, and withdrawing your hands without commanding, "Out!"

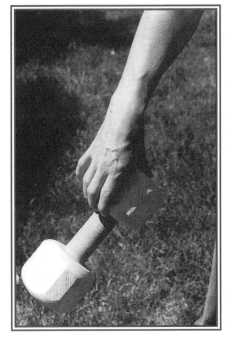

The grasp for throwing the dumbbell so it's less likely to bounce off-line.

or taking the object. Praise, "Good bring!" as Pooch continues to hold on. Should he drop it, confusion is the issue, not disobedience. Gently say, "No, no" and give him the dumbbell. Then repeat the tap exercise, praising your friend as he holds on.

THE THROW

The ideal toss causes the dumbbell to land without bouncing far away or to a side. Hold the end between your thumb and fingers. Position your thumb directly behind the block and curl your fingers over the front, with your knuckles toward the direction you intend to throw. Though it may feel awkward at first, this grip causes a dumbbell to back-spin and die where it lands. Practice without Pooch nearby, so you don't have to inhibit enthusiasm by restraining him from chasing the object.

REFLECTION

Quit now, you'll never make it. If you disregard this advice, you'll be halfway there.

DAVID ZUCKER

RETRIEVING OVER THE HIGH JUMP

EASY JUMP-RETRIEVING TRAINING

You may be able to start this work simply by tossing a dumbbell over a jump and commanding, "Hup! Bring!" Given the earlier jumping-at-heel work and the retrieving lessons so far, your pet may get the idea and respond properly. If not, start at the beginning, as follows.

RETRIEVE OVER HIGH JUMP: METHODICAL TEACHING

Begin the first day's session with a flat retrieve followed by a recall over the jump, to set up your dog's mind. If Pooch doesn't perform well, work out problem areas before continuing.

Then set the jump's height even with your dog's elbows. "Sit!" your dog in front of and facing the jump from eight feet. Have him take and hold a dumbbell. Command, "Stay!" and walk to the jump's opposite side, preferably by stepping over it (to suggest the correct route). Stand facing your dog within touching distance of the jump. As one flowing action slap the top board's edge, command, "Bring! Hup!" and back away to create landing room. Repeat the lesson three times and end today's session.

The front-and-facing sit needn't be perfect today, and skip the finish for now. Were your pet to make a mistake, you'd have to accept sloppy work or correct him during a new lesson, a lesser-of-evils choice.

The next day, with Pooch at heel, throw the dumbbell over the jump, sending him as it lands by pointing toward the jump and commanding, "Hup!" "Bring!" and "Hup!" The first "Hup!" sends the animal and "Bring!" should be timed while he's airborne, going for the dumbbell. Use the second "Hup!" right after the dog picks up the object. Now your task is phasing out commands and gestures used only

Teaching the retrieve over high jump is little more than a recombination of previously learned skills.

for teaching, waiting a few seconds before sending the dog after the dumbbell and gradually raising the jump to the proper competition height.

If Pooch resists during this training stage, the message is his retrieving foundation is shaky and should be strengthened. He's been brought too far too fast.

COMPETITION JUMP HEIGHT

The required jump height in 4-H (as an example) is your dog's height at the withers. Don't jump your companion at full height until he is at least a year old. His skeleton must be ready to safely absorb the impacts of landing.

REFLECTION

One of the great things in this world is not so much where we are, but in what direction we are moving.

OLIVER WENDELL HOLMES

25 THE BROAD JUMP

THE SIMPLEST OBSTACLE?

The broad jump can be deceptive in its simplicity. It seems uncomplicated on paper, but its true ease lies in how many ways a dog can perform it incorrectly. My advice is to delay teaching the broad jump until your pal is an experienced jumper.

CONFIGURATION

During initial teaching, arrange the jump as a stacked formation: two boards placed horizontally on their edges, parallel to one another and eight inches apart; and two boards set horizontally on their flat sides, atop and at slight angles to the first two boards. If your pet would be more likely to crawl over this setup than jump it, alter the pattern to one less tempting.

TEACHING

The first step, taking Pooch over the broad jump at heel, is no different from heeling over any new obstacle. "Fuss!" toward the jump and command, "Hup!" as you both leap over it, praising, "Good hup!" after landing. Repeat this over-broad-jump-at-heel procedure three times before progressing.

Next, recall your pet over the formation. After four days of broad jump recalls, start lengthening the setup a few inches daily, eventually extending it to the correct length (twice the dog's competition high jump height) and layout. For reasons that will become clear, after leaving Pooch in preparation to commanding him over the jump, always walk along the jump's right side.

The last step is formatting broad jump work according to how it's performed in Open obedience classes. The handler leaves his or her

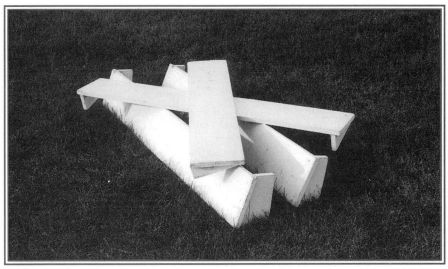

The idea behind initially configuring the broad jump as shown is to prevent your dog from learning to walk through it, a habit that's difficult to eradicate later.

The first step in teaching the broad jump is heeling your dog toward the obstacle, which is in stacked configuration, and jumping over it with the dog.

The next step in teaching the broad jump is recalling your pet over the obstacle, lengthening its dimension a few inches daily until it approximates the full distance your dog is required to jump in competition.

dog on a sit-stay facing and at least eight feet from the broad jump. He or she walks to a point along the right side of the hurdles and faces them from two feet. When cued by the judge, the handler commands Pooch to jump, turning toward the landing area while the dog is airborne.

Adapt the procedure via two simple steps. First, following a recall over the hurdle, set your dog up for a second recall. Command, "Hup!" but this time, as soon as he's in the air (not before), hurriedly back leftward into position alongside the hurdles, facing the spot where your companion will land.

After a few days take the second step. Conduct the exercise once, as you've been doing. Then "Stay!" your pet for a repeat performance. Leave, but instead of moving to the jump's opposite end and turning to face the animal, command, "Hup!" *as you're passing the right edge of the hurdles.* Accompany the command with a forward, sweeping gesture with your left arm. What's left is gradually altering the procedure to stopping at the jump's right before "Hup!" and phasing out the signal.

The handler backs into the correct ring position while her dog is jumping.

ANTICIPATION PROBLEMS

Anticipation difficulties, such as jumping before being commanded, can be eliminated by preceding "Hup!" with an infrequent and unexpected "Platz!" Command your partner to lie down from the sit-stay, then send him over the broad jump. Another idea is leaving the dog in a sit-stay at the end of the jump, and, after walking to the obstacle's right side, return without commanding, "Hup!" The intent common to both methods is to break the pattern, saying to your pal he must wait for your cue; that your next command cannot and should not be predicted.

THE WALKER

The greatest difficulty in teaching the broad jump is had by trainers whose animals have learned to walk across or through the hurdles. From a dog's perspective, the broad jump would be more easily negotiated by walking through or over it. The high jump and, to a degree, the bar jump suggest a need for leaving the ground. The broad jump doesn't. This is why broad jump work is best taught only to a reliable jumper.

To cure the problem, first drop the exercise for several weeks or months, depending on the difficulty's severity and duration. This lessens faulty memory traces, and is preferable to trying to override

The leash is a useful tool in many instances.

them while they're fresh and strong. Then restart the training, using a new method and a different command; using the old command can trigger old habits.

CENTERING

A second broad jump difficulty is the possibility that a dog may jump toward a front corner, often the one nearer the handler. The upright-post design of the high jump, as well as the handler's location relative to the obstacle, usually drives a dog to jump center. The broad jump's center definition is more vague.

Off-center jumping can often be trained out simply by placing a leash across the corner being cut (most dogs won't jump over their own lead). Accompany leash placement with much eye contact.

Another helpful technique is placing high jump supports at both sides of the broad jump's midway point. This helps define or at least suggest the broad jump's centerline.

REFLECTION

People are always blaming their circumstances for what they are. I don't believe in circumstances. The people who get on in this world are the people who get up and look for the circumstances they want, and, if they can't find them, make them.

GEORGE BERNARD SHAW

OBEDIENCE: UTILITY

26 HAND SIGNALS

PLUSES AND MINUSES

Hand signal work is simple material for trainers, and dogs generally learn signals easier and quicker than spoken commands. This is logical from the canine perspective—audible cues play a minor part in the dog's world, as dogs naturally communicate a great deal through body language. As any knowledgeable breeder can attest, an assertive dam's withering glance can check an exuberant puppy's rowdy behavior and stop it cold in its tracks.

One pitfall of signals is that a handler can lapse in concentration and inadvertently cue his or her dog. A trainer can unconsciously adjust eyeglasses, scratch an itch, alter posture and so forth, and then wonder why Pooch suddenly broke an obedience sequence.

A positive aspect of signals is increased attention on the handler. A dog learns it must keep an eye on number one. An even greater plus is that signals heighten bonding. Since the cues occur at a more intimate level, dogs view them as more personal than spoken commands—the rest of the world doesn't get to hear.

TRAINING GUIDELINES

Introduce any signal only after running the dog through the exercise under verbal command, to set up his mind.

Teach each signal only after Pooch is adept at the exercise under voice command, so he has a sound in mind—a mental label, so to speak—to associate with the signal.

When teaching signals, remain silent throughout the session (I'll mention exceptions as we go along). As signaled commands are silent, so praise and correction should be nonverbal. Repeated switching between voice and signals during teaching can cloud a lesson.

Teach signals in the order presented. Don't progress to the next signal until your dog is solid on the one before it.

To ensure control, work on leash unless otherwise directed.

"WHAT IF HE DIDN'T SEE ME?"

Once your pet has the idea that you sometimes command with your hands, don't delay a signal until he glances your way. The teacher decides when a command is to be given—not the student. Using stay as an example, give the signal and leave; if Pooch also departs, having inattentively missed the signal, correct for the broken stay and leave again. If the dog seems confused, repeat the signal when leaving the second time. True, commands, whether spoken or signaled, should not be repeated; but when clarity of intent is on the line, theoretical ideals must defer to practical considerations.

STAY

The stay signal is taught in much the same manner as the voice command. Give the palm-over-the-eyes stay signal and step away briefly a short distance. Return and praise silently: brief petting, flash the stay signal, more quick petting, give the signal again and still more petting. This technique clarifies the reason for your praise. Increase distance and time at the same rate for the spoken stay (see chapter 11, "*Training Session Three*").

FIRST SIGNAL?

A point I could have mentioned earlier may have more meaning now—stay isn't the first signal you've taught. Granted, it's the first hand signal, but signal work began when you taught automatic sit during on-leash heeling—Pooch learned to take your ending of motion to be a sit signal.

HEELING

With your dog sitting at heel, flip your left hand forward and start walking. Though the chances a dog might balk are slight, encouragingly pat your left leg and repeat the signal if needed. Silently praise by brief petting as you walk, assuming your dog is tall enough that you can reach him while walking. Otherwise, a smile and nods of your head will have to do, and they will be enough.

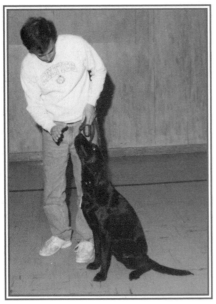

The "Stay!" hand signal.

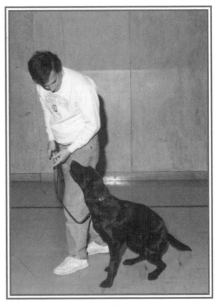

The hand signal for heeling.

STAND FROM MOTION

Begin teaching this exercise by signaling "Fuss!" Stop after a few paces and give and continue to hold the stand signal: your right palm in front of Pooch's eyes. If needed, lightly touch the outside flank with your left hand, or, if you're training a small dog, scoot your left foot underneath its midsection to freeze it in position. Return the signaling hand to your side and, before your pet can move, give the stay signal. Move away briefly a short distance. Gradually increase duration and distance until the working range is twenty feet for as long as it takes you to walk that far, count to ten and return.

DOWN FROM THE STAND

This signal is covered in chapter 19, *"Drop on Recall,"* under the sub-heading *"Down at a Distance."*

SIT FROM DOWN

To teach this signal—an upward, sweeping, left-hand motion—first signal platz from two or three feet. Once the animal is grounded, signal

Teaching the hand signal for the stand from motion. I prefer the right hand for this signal, as using the left increases the likelihood of accidentally touching the dog, which can cost points.

The hand signal for the down from either the sitting or the standing position. Note how the Labrador's attention stays on the trainer as the animal goes to ground.

sit as you take a very quick, long step toward it. Your motion will likely cause the sit, but temporarily add the spoken "Sit!" to aid understanding. Praise, "Good sit," as your pet rises. Once he gets the idea, gradually lessen your step-toward-the-dog movement until you can phase out the gesture altogether.

RECALL

The recall signal is a quick, right-handed gesture toward your midsection. Leave the dog on a signaled sit-stay and step to leash's end. Signal the recall and run backward, as you did when teaching the exercise verbally. Praise silently by petting Pooch's chin when he arrives and sits. A perfectly straight front-sit is currently of minor importance—work on that once the dog is doing well with the recall signal. After three days, begin lessening backward movement and start increasing distance.

The recall hand signal.

The hand signal for the sit from the down.

The hand signal for either the inside or the flip finish. If you prefer the outside finish, use your right hand.

FINISH

Verbally run through the finish two or three times in rapid succession. Then do so once using only the signal, a hand flip to indicate direction (for the inside finish, signal with the left hand; for the outside finish, use the right). Initially add appropriate body language—turning your upper body toward the finish direction—phasing out the mannerism as Pooch learns.

REFLECTION

Learning the value of silence is learning to listen to, instead of screaming at, reality: opening your mind enough to find what the end of someone's sentence sounds like, or listening to a dog until you discover what is needed instead of imposing yourself in the name of training.

THOMAS DOBUSH

CHAPTER 97

DIRECTED RETRIEVING

TEACHING THE DIRECTED RETRIEVE

Directed retrieving finds a dog fetching a specific item while ignoring other nearby similar items. Teaching begins by having Pooch fetch a thrown dumbbell, the purpose being to put him in a retrieving frame of mind. Next, have him retrieve a thrown white cloth glove, after first allowing the animal to sniff and otherwise examine it. If he shows any reluctance or nervousness toward the object—a highly unlikely response—cure the problem via play activities with the glove before proceeding.

Command, "Sit! Stay!" then walk four paces in the direction your dog is facing and place the glove on the ground. Return to the heel position, point toward the glove and command, "Bring!"

If Pooch displays any confusion over what's expected, walk him to the article and encourage through word and gesture. If resistance causes him to hold back—an extremely remote possibility at this stage—it's probable he's been brought too far too fast. Revert to dumbbell retrieving until he's past contention.

Following four days of retrieving a single glove four times daily, start the following sequence. Begin a session with another placed-glove retrieve. Then command, "Sit! Stay!" and go drop the glove once more. Instead of returning, though, drop a second glove a few feet to the left. Go to your pal, command, "Fuss!" and turn to your left and halt, aiming you and pooch toward the new glove. (If you'd rather do a nearly full turn to the right in place to face your dog toward the second glove, do so.) Point at the new glove and command, "Bring!"

If pooch steps toward the first glove, immediately block him with your body and guide him to the correct article. If he seems confused,

First teach your dog to retrieve a single glove.

Block your dog rather than correct him should he start for the wrong glove.

stay with single-glove retrieves for a few more days before starting the two-gloves format.

Most dogs will retrieve the correct glove. Presuming your worker is in this majority, praise, "Good bring!" as he returns. Take the glove and switch from approval to "Fuss!" aligning pooch toward the first glove. Then command him to fetch it.

Four days later, set gloves at north, east, south and west, with your companion observing the placements. Have your dog retrieve them one at a time. Keep the retrieving order random; avoid establishing a pattern Pooch might figure out. After a week at this level, install the ring format by working with only three gloves, gradually adjusting the location of the outside two until all are in a line perpendicular to your starting location.

The next step in teaching the directed retrieve is to place gloves at the compass points.

REFLECTION

Never esteem anything as of advantage to you that will make you break your word or lose your self-respect.

MARCUS AURELIUS
ANTONINUS

CHAPTER 28

SCENT RETRIEVING

OVERVIEW

A scent retriever fetches a handler-scented article from among similar but unscented objects. Trainers who haven't taught scent retrieving sometimes approach the work nervously. Beginning students, after watching a dog perform the exercise, often react that it must be extremely challenging training. Most Utility Dog trainers I've met, though, feel the work is often easier to perfect than precision heeling. I agree.

Competitors should know that scent retrieving can be taught to untitled dogs without causing confusion over pre–Utility Dog requirements. However, don't work with a dog not solid on the retrieve on the flat and the retrieve over high jump. Also, don't train scenting while teaching directed retrieving, the send-away or tracking. You want to work with a seasoned, "all-aspects" retriever; you don't want to risk confusion with other "Move away from me" exercises like the send-away, or similar yet different nose work, like tracking.

Choice of teaching method depends on the dog's bonding level and how he best learns. My rapport method is based on natural handler-dog communication and is loosely structured. My structured method is more systematized and, though rapport plays a part, it does so to a lesser degree. Some dogs more readily absorb information when it's presented in a highly formatted manner. Others do as well, often better, by diving into the middle of things—just as we do.

SCENT RETRIEVING: RAPPORT METHOD

Because dogs are more drawn to natural articles than to manufactured items, start by placing five twigs (chips of bark work equally well) in an area measuring three feet square. Train on a surfaced area instead of a lawn, which can give off distracting scents. Wear rubber kitchen gloves when handling the scent-retrieve articles to avoid scenting any, and place them so that no two touch each other. Scent one thoroughly by putting it inside your shirt and leash up your dog.

Heel to a point six feet from the nearest article. After pooch's auto-sit, command, "Stay!" and take the scented object from your shirt. Flip the scent article in the air a few times to capture attention. Pass it once under your pet's nose, remind, "Stay!" and walk to the unscented articles. Place the scented item near the others so you can be sure of its location. Return to your dog, pass your hand near his nose and repeatedly command, "Find it!" while gesturing encouragingly toward the articles. Follow slightly behind your worker as he approaches the objects; you should be nearby but not so close as to distract.

When nearing anything of interest, almost any dog lowers his head to examine it. (The dog that shows little interest should be encouraged by voice and gesture; he shouldn't be forced.) As he inspects the scent items, softly praise, "Good!" If he tries to pick up an incorrect article, gently say, "No, no" while guiding him from it. When he sniffs the right one, regardless of how he reacts to it, instantly respond excitedly, "Good find it! Bring!" Repeat, "Bring!" as many times as needed.

At this point, every dog to which I've taught this exercise has done two things. First, he has jerked his head up and looked at me, displaying what I call the "Moment of Recognition"—that flash when a dog's aspect says, "Aha! I see what my trainer wants!" After my "Good find it! Bring!" response to his searching, wide-eyed look, the animal has done the second thing: grabbed the object and proudly walked toward me.

Pet your dog, tell him what a "Good find it!" he did and lead him from the training area, allowing him to carry his prize if he wishes. End the session to guarantee finishing high, which would be at risk were the routine repeated. When you do "Out!" the article, use only minimal force in taking it should Pooch fail to release. Don't risk dampening enthusiasm through force.

After three similar training sessions, switch to placing the scented object among the others *before* bringing your pet to the area. A week later, begin using ring articles by substituting them for whatever items you've been using. Should your dog resist the formal articles, insert them inside individual cloth gloves to make them more dog-acceptable. Then follow the program outlined in step 5 below, "Conclude Transfer to Ring Scent Articles," and step 6, "Format Routine to Ring Specifications."

SCENT RETRIEVING: STRUCTURED METHOD

STEP 1: SEEK BACK

Begin teaching the seek back by placing four cloth gloves inside your shirt to scent them heavily. Without letting your dog know you have them, bring him on leash to the training area (use a leather or cloth collar today). Then heel straight ahead and drop a glove behind you as you walk. Drop it right-handed, with your companion unaware you dropped anything. A few paces later turn around, continue walking and bring your hand under his nose. Repeat, "Find it!" while pointing toward the glove and leading your retriever toward it.

As he approaches and sniffs, investigates and perhaps pounces upon the article, praise, "Good find it!" Pocket the glove and continue heeling.

Several paces later drop another glove, again without your pet being aware you've done so. As before, take a few more steps, turn around, bring your hand under Pooch's beak and command, "Find it!" He may try to pull you to it (that's why we don't want to use a choker or a pinch collar today); let him. Praise, "Good find it! Bring!" as you back away encouragingly, take the glove and continue heeling. Repeat the entire procedure twice more, then take your pal from the training area, marveling at his dandy find. The next three sessions are repeats of this one.

STEP 2: BEGIN TRANSFER TO RING ARTICLES

You need two sets of formal utility articles, numbered one through five but otherwise identical. One set should be metal, the other leather. Of the three styles commonly available, I prefer the two-bar style, as it keeps one bar elevated, making it easier for most dogs to pick up.

The idea is to now use utility articles instead of gloves during seek back work. Begin with metal articles, because if a dog resists a utility object it will probably be one of the metal items, not the leather ones. It's better to deal with any resistance now, not after a preference for the leather articles has been established.

Make the transfer through one of two ways, depending on which approach you feel will be easier for your pet. The first is inserting a metal article into a scented glove; the second is simply to start using metal articles in place of gloves.* This step might appear to offer unnecessary haste to the progression, but some very successful trainers claim it's the only way to go. If you make the transition to ring articles directly and see that the new items bother your dog, immediately switch to inserting the articles into gloves. However, should Pooch indicate he's simply not going to pick up "that thing," be it covered or not, attach a pincher and correct as for any retrieve refusal.**

Remain for four days at this level: four six- to fifteen-foot, daily seek backs of metal, glove-enshrouded scent articles, or of metal articles alone.

STEP 3: PRE-LOCATE ARTICLES

This step constitutes a minor yet significant change. Place four gloved (or plain) scented articles, each ten feet apart, in a straight line *before* bringing Pooch to the training area. Command, "Find it!" as you enter the site and accompany your dog to the first object. After taking it from him, continue until all have been found and end the session.

STEP 4: ADDITION OF UNSCENTED ARTICLES

If you've already eliminated the gloves, ignore references to them in the following outline.

Several days before starting this phase, set out three gloves and three metal articles to air, to eliminate any residual scent. Remember to wear rubber kitchen gloves when handling them, to avoid accidentally scenting one.

Days later, create a fourth article-in-glove combination, after first heavily scenting the target article and glove by rubbing them with your hands. Tuck the package in your shirt and put on your kitchen gloves. Gather up the three nonscented article-within-glove combinations, taking care not to touch them barehanded. Proceed to the training area *without* your dog.

Position the unscented articles in a triangular pattern, setting each one three feet apart. Place the scented article/glove three feet to one side from the unscented ones. Locate the scented item so that wind won't carry scent from it to the unscented ones. Then escort your dog to the yard.

---

*I'd just as soon go for broke with a full scent layout (and have been known to do so) as risk confusion in the training sequence, but this gets into the area where only you can know your pet's tendencies best.

**See chapter 22, *"Retrieving on the Flat,"* under the section "You Put It There—You Pick It Up!"

Walk your pet toward an unscented article. Send a message along the leash by making the approach akin to stalking prey: crouched, sneaking along slowly and deliberately, encouraging Pooch in excited whispers to, "Find it!"

As he nears the first nonscented combination, doubtless he'll sniff it. If he doesn't, in fact, make certain you haven't leashed up the family cat by mistake. Keep silent as he scents, so as not to distract. He will either turn away or attempt to pick up the article. Should he turn away, guide him toward the next unscented article, still urging, "Find it!"

During this process, don't let your dog pick up a nonscented article. Allow a couple of sniffs, then move him along before he has an opportunity to scoop up the object. If he tries to pick up a nonscented combination before you can move him from it, block him, or, if you're too late, command, "Out!" and gently take the object from him. Remember: When a dog investigates something like this, he normally sniffs it, stares at it for a blink or two and takes it with his mouth if he feels like picking up the object. It's during that second or two of staring that you must guide him from the nonscented article.

At the second nonscented article, your pet may seem confused. Having not had success, he may be unable to see what's expected of him. If you sense any confusion, skip going to the third unscented article/glove. Go instead to the scented one, encouraging as before, "Find it!"

As you and Pooch near the scented article, stand where your dog can see you without having to turn from the object (so not to strain his concentration). Watch closely as his nose goes down—be alert for that moment of recognition. While it's sometimes very subtle, often it's characterized by the animal suddenly freezing all motion, after first snapping his head back slightly from the article, then by either looking at you searchingly (for confirmation), or literally pouncing upon the object. In either case your response must be emphatic and sincere: "Yes! Good find it!" Add, "Bring!" while pointing toward the object if your companion seems unsure whether to grab it.

Lead your dog from the area. Let him carry his trophy if he wishes, and comment along the way how impressed you are with his "Good find it!" End on this high point, rather than risk overriding it with less successful experiences that could happen if you were to continue. Congratulate yourself, too: You've accomplished much.

Continue this training sequence for the next three days, each day placing the scented article in a different location relative to the unscented ones—don't unintentionally teach Pooch to key on a visual pattern.

STEP 5: CONCLUDE TRANSFER TO RING SCENT ARTICLES

After four consecutive successful days of retrieving scented, article-within-glove combinations, begin this phase by using scissors and imagination. The objective is to gradually reduce the glove's size. Start by snipping off the fingers. Over the next few sessions, remove a bit more until only wristbands remain.

Then avoid any scent work for a few days. During the layoff, concentrate on some activity your dog truly enjoys, like chasing his play toy. The idea is to take his thoughts further from specific memories of scent articles in combination with gloves. Then return to scent retrieving where you left off, except you should no longer use gloves or portions of them. Four days after restarting, add leather articles.

STEP 6: FORMAT ROUTINE TO RING SPECIFICATIONS

Effect four modifications over the next few weeks. First, begin grouping the articles together, but no closer than eight inches from each other, the minimum ring distance. Second, gradually increase the distance Pooch covers to the articles until he's starting from thirty feet. Third, work on grassy areas, to accustom your pet to shutting out the natural odors he will encounter in the ground. Last, condition him to sit quietly at heel while a helper moves several feet behind you, acting as a ring official placing a scented article among the nonscented ones. (The helper should use tongs handling the article you've scented, so as not to add his or her own scent.)

VARIATIONS

NUMBER ONE

If for any reason Pooch simply doesn't get the idea of scent retrieving, make one subtle training adjustment. Initially teach him to seek his own scent. Use either the rapport method or the structured method, as follows.

When a dog experiences uncommon difficulty with any exercise, drop the work for several weeks to allow fading of faulty memories. Then, in this instance, start the new approach using three matched wooden dumbbells and a new command (like "Seek it!")

Have your dog retrieve a dumbbell on flat ground twice, to load the object with his scent and yours. Leaving your pal on a stay, hide the article several yards away, either in tall grass, behind a tree, among leaves or under a shallow covering of snow, to prevent your dog from seeing where you placed the object. Return to your pet, heel to within a few feet of the dumbbell and command, "Seek it!" while pointing toward the object's location. Praise, "Good seek it!" as he picks up the dumbbell. Take it, command, "Stay!" and hide it again but in a different location. Have the dog "Seek it!" again. Repeat this hide-the-dumbbell/"Seek it!" drill twice more and end the session. If he wants, allow your dog to carry the dumbbell as you leave the training area.

The next three training periods are the same as this one, including having Pooch retrieve the dumbbell once or twice at the start of each session. Use the same dumbbell throughout these practices, to saturate it with as much of your scent as possible.

Begin the next phase by placing two similar dumbbells three feet apart before bringing your dog to the training area. Wear rubber kitchen gloves when handling the items so as not to scent them. Bring your budding genius to the training site and have him fetch the dumbbell you've been using. When throwing it, though, hurl it directly away from where you've placed the other dumbbells. "Out!" the object, command, "Stay!" and place it three feet from the dumbbells set out earlier. Return to your dog, attach the leash (for control) and say, "Seek it!"

As your pet inspects the items, softly praise, "Good!" If he tries to pick up a dumbbell other than the correct one, gently say, "No, no," while guiding him from it. When Pooch sniffs the right one, regardless of how he reacts to it, instantly respond excitedly, "Good seek it! Bring!"

Pet your dog, telling him what a "Good seek it!" he did, and take him from the training area, allowing him to carry his prize if he wishes. End the session to finish high, which further work could threaten.

After three similar training sessions, switch to placing the scented dumbbell among the others *before* bringing your pet to the site. A week later, change to using ring articles by substituting them for the dumbbells you've been using.

NUMBER TWO

A good friend had breezed through the first two levels of AKC obedience competition with his Golden Retriever, earning High in Trial honors their first time out. When it came to scent retrieving, however, the dog simply didn't get the word.

My friend decided to raise the target article's scent level. He rubbed a piece of bologna on the target dumbbell, then smeared the meat on his hands. As he later told me, "I walked pooch to a point near the articles, had him sniff my hand, he then sniffed the dumbbell I had polished with the bologna, and you talk about 'moment of recognition!' His eyes liked to bug out of his head." They went on to win the coveted Utility Dog title without mishap.

REFLECTION

Procrastination is the fear of success. People procrastinate because they are afraid of the success that they know will result if they move ahead now. Because success is heavy, carries a responsibility with it, it is much easier to procrastinate and live on the "someday I'll . . ." philosophy.

DENIS WAITLEY

CHAPTER 29   THE SEND-AWAY

In a send-away routine (also called a send-out or go-out), a Utility Dog (UD) handler commands his or her sitting dog away and, as the animal nears the ring's opposite side, commands, "Sit!" The handler then cues the dog to return over one of two jumps: the standard high jump or the bar jump. After clearing the hurdle, the dog sits in the front-and-facing position, finishing when commanded. The exercise is repeated, but this time the dog returns via the jump that wasn't used the first time.

Because competition demands structured consistency, my method of teaching the UD send-away is to target the dog on the ring environment itself. This requires creating a ring setting at your training site. That's not to say you must duplicate a UD ring, complete with judge, stewards, fencing and crowd. If need be, clothesline strung between two trees to represent one side of the ring can serve. The two jumps should be present, but they shouldn't be set up during this teaching stage. They're merely equipment on hand, waiting in jumbled heaps to be erected. Don't draw attention to their presence; that could distract Pooch from the business at hand.

Locate the best go-out termination point in your contrived ring setting. This spot is midway along the side having the fewest distractions. Then determine your starting point, which is directly across the ring from the termination point.

For today's training, use a leather or cloth collar with a tab attached. Put on a jacket, pocket a tennis ball and lead your dog on leash to your starting point.

Leaving your pet in whichever stay he's most reliable, remove your lead and walk to the ring's opposite side. Place your jacket (or other outer garment) on the ground where your dog can easily see it. Return to your pal, point at the jacket, command, "Run!" and quickly escort him to it. Should curiosity drive the dog to drag you to the object, so much the better—an inquisitive attitude makes training easier.

The Send-Away.

Hold the collar tab while approaching the jacket. Convince Pooch he's being (mildly) restrained from going ahead to investigate. The purpose is to cause your pet to drive forward (as you know, when you pull a dog one way he tends to pull the other way), but skip the technique if you feel it might confuse or inhibit. A few feet from the jacket, release the tab while again commanding, "Run!" and pointing toward the garment.

After the animal arrives at the target, allow a few seconds for investigation, then command, "Sit!" (Permit this exploration period only during the first session; prevent later investigations by commanding, "Sit!" upon arrival.) As your dog sits, immediately produce the tennis ball (which I assume to be your pet's favorite toy) from the jacket's pocket and throw the toy for him. The purposes are to say what fun it is to dash to the target, and that Pooch is wise to rivet attention on you upon arrival to be ready to play.

Praise as your dog returns with the ball, take it from him, repeat the entire sequence three times and take the dog from the area. Encourage the animal to carry the toy but don't force the issue.

The next three sessions are identical to this one.

SHOULD MATTERS GO AWRY

Suggestions for dealing with selected problems are discussed below.

Problem: You've taken your pet on leash to your starting point, but today's heeling is a disaster.
Solution: Get the animal's mind right about "Fuss!"; take him from the area and try again tomorrow.

Problem: Your dog significantly breaks the stay while you walk to the ring's opposite side.
Solution: Correct him. Make him hold the stay as you proceed to the ring's other side. Return after a few seconds, praise, take him from the yard and restart the go-out tomorrow.

Problem: After you release the tab while again commanding, "Run!" and pointing toward the article, the dog's response is to stand there and stare at you.
Solution: Run him to the garment, using encouragement rather than force. When the two of you arrive, command, "Sit!" and continue the sequence.

Problem: After the animal has arrived at the target, he has forgotten the meaning of "Sit!"
Solution: Repeat, "Sit!" Repeating commands is out of place with an experienced dog, but this one is just learning the

work; besides, the sit is secondary to the primary goal of teaching the go-out. But if repeating the command has no effect, refresh your dog's memory through mild correction and continue.

Problem: After you've thrown the ball for your dog, he moves slightly from the sit-stay in anticipation of chasing the ball.
Solution: Forget it. It's too minor a goof to bother with at this point. Toss the toy and continue.

Problem: Your dog doesn't return with the ball.
Solution: Encourage your pet. This difficulty is rarely encountered at this stage.

CHANGES

After completing the first four training sessions, there are two short-term goals. First is to send-out the dog without having to walk him as far as was necessary the day before. The second is commanding, "Sit!" at ever-increasing distances.

To accomplish the first objective, simply stop walking at successively farther distances from the target. Should your pet respond by going part way and stopping, confusion is more likely the problem than defiance. He may be wondering why you didn't run the distance with him as before. Stepping forward and giving encouragement is a better solution than correction. However, if Pooch resists you, grasp the collar tab and correct via a series of quick jerks accompanied by, "Run! Run! Run!" while gesturing toward the target. Reattach the pinch collar if needed. Likewise, if at any point your "Sit!" command is ignored, let your dog know through appropriate correction that you aren't buying it. That type of canine amnesia rarely arises from confusion.

Once your pet will go-out unaccompanied to the article, make the following adjustment. Drape a small, easily visible cloth over the ring rope above the target, making certain the activity isn't lost on your dog. Return and continue the lesson.

After four sessions make another change. Set out the jacket and the cloth target before bringing Pooch to the training site. Four days later, stop using the clothing article altogether but continue to hang a small piece of cloth over the ring rope before bringing your companion to the training area. Starting four days later, reduce the size of the cloth over a period of days until it ceases to exist. Also during this time-of-the-shrinking-cloth, erect the jumps to Pooch's current working height. Set up the equipment over several days (a little at a time) and without your dog present, to avoid calling any special attention to the jump's presence. Add directed jumping (see chapter 21) when Pooch is solid on the send-away.

When practicing the entire go-out routine, alter which jump you first send your pal over. Don't teach a pattern of always commanding it over the bar jump first, for example. That can cause ring problems if a judge initially directs you to send your dog over the high jump.

REFLECTION

We should be careful to get out of an experience only the wisdom that is in it—and stop there; lest we be like the cat that sits down on a hot stove lid. She will never sit down on a hot stove lid again—and that is well; but also she will never sit down on a cold one anymore.

MARK TWAIN

30

STAND FROM MOTION/ RECALL TO HEEL

In the stand from motion/recall to heel, the judge directs a handler, "Stand your dog," during off-leash heeling. The handler cues his or her dog to stand-stay, continues walking about ten paces and turns to face his or her dog (the handler does not stop next to the animal when commanding the stand-stay). The judge extensively "goes over" the animal and instructs the handler to call the dog directly to heel, not to the conventional front-and-facing position.

STAND FROM MOTION: MEDIUM TO LARGE DOGS

Begin with your dog in the heel position and hold the leash right-handed. While walking at a normal pace, command, "Wait!" and apply light, left-handed fingertip pressure to the left flank. Don't grasp the flank, merely touch it. This technique stops most dogs in their tracks.

Be sure to touch the left (outside) flank, not the one nearer you. Touching the inside flank can cause a dog to move his hindquarters away from the handler, a reaction that would defeat our goal of an instantaneous stand from motion.

It's usually not necessary to remain next to the dog once he's halted, but do so at first if it seems unsure or nervous about this development. After he stops, give the stay hand signal. Don't accompany it with the spoken "Stay!"; Pooch might react to the "S" sound by sitting.

STAND FROM MOTION: SMALL DOGS

Teach the stand along a fence or a similar barrier next to the animal's left. Because you operate from his right, having an obstacle to his left prevents the dog from shying away, which he could otherwise do during the following lessons.

Warm up with some heeling. Then command, "Fuss!" once more and, after a few steps, command, "Wait!" At the same instant, stop and slide your left foot under your pal's midsection. Use the instep to position him.

The maneuver is difficult, not only from the standpoint of coordination and balance but because it must be done smoothly so as not to scare the animal. Practice it by yourself until you feel comfortable trying it with your dog.

With any size of dog, looping a second leash around the animal's girth can be helpful in reinforcing "Wait!" Avoid collar pressure, though—that can cause a dog to sit.

RECALL TO HEEL: TEACHING

This is nothing more than a finish from a distance. Leave your pet on a six-foot, on-leash stand-stay. Call him with "Fuss!" (not with "Here!"). Repeat the command as needed and guide him to the heel position. Add distance until Pooch is reliable at thirty feet.

Do *not* teach this work before completing other obedience levels—they require a front sit before the finish.

REFLECTION

Do not be too timid and squeamish about your actions. All life is an experiment.

Ralph Waldo Emerson

OBEDIENCE: SHOWING

31 RULES AND PROCEDURES

In general, community-sponsored competition is open to all purebred or mixed-breed dogs in good health. A dog that limps, is blind, deaf or is similarly afflicted—or a bitch in season—cannot be shown. Whether an animal has been neutered is not a consideration.

To earn a qualifying score, which makes you and Pooch eligible for further competition, you must win at least 170 of the two hundred points available at each competition level. Also, more than half of the points for each exercise must be won. Scoring fifteen points in a thirty-point routine is not a qualifying total; earning sixteen or more points for the same routine is.

Except for the stays, all routines are individual. You, your dog and the judge are in the ring by yourselves, except for ring stewards (helpers) during activities requiring their presence. After the dog-handler teams complete the individual exercises, stays are performed in groups, each group being known as a *Class*.* Unless excused by the judge, all competitors must return for the stays, regardless of each's performance so far.

No dog may be carried in the ring, but you may praise your pet between exercises. Since dogs must be under "reasonable control" at all times, keep praise light while in the ring. Lively praise can excite a dog, and if Pooch responds by jumping on you, he may be considered not to be under "reasonable control."

*A large class may be divided for the stays.

CATEGORIES

Obedience is divided into six levels:

First Year

On Leash

Novice

Graduate Novice

Open

Utility

Each level (except First Year) is split into categories "A" and "B." "A" is for students who have never successfully competed at a specific level. "B" students are those who have earned a qualifying score at that level with another dog, or whose pets were trained to that level by someone else. This can occur in families where dogs are something akin to hand-me-downs.

A student can compete at any level without completing those ahead of it, but a student cannot drop from one level to another with the same dog. For example, a youngster who competes in Graduate Novice cannot later show the same dog in Novice. The same animal could be shown in Novice "B" by another student, however, such as a brother or sister. The person who originally trained the dog could show another dog in Novice "B."

GENERAL

At all levels the judge directs each student through the exercises. The judge begins each routine with, "Are you ready?" and ends with, "Exercise finished." When asked if you're ready, look and make sure you and your pet really are ready before answering, "Yes," because from that moment you're being judged. If your dog isn't sitting or is sitting crooked, for example, command, "Sit!" or align the animal first.

HEEL AND FIGURE EIGHT

At all levels the judge uses the following instructions for a heeling pattern: "Forward," "Right turn," "Left turn," "About turn," "Fast," "Slow," "Normal," and "Halt" or "Stop," though not necessarily in that order. During the figure eight, the judge directs, "Forward," and "Halt" or "Stop."

The following list defines each instruction.

Forward: Heel your dog, starting forward (around the posts during the figure eight).

Right turn and **left turn**: Turn ninety degrees to your right or your left.

About turn: Turn around; go in the other direction. About turns are made to the right.

Fast: Run, not walk fast.

Slow: Walk *very* slowly.

Normal: Walk at your normal pace.

Halt or **stop**: Stop walking and stand still.

You may hold your leash in either hand but not in both hands.

Make turns, speed changes and stops normally. I've seen handlers react to, "Halt," for instance, by nearly toppling over from abruptly slamming on the brakes. Respond to instructions promptly but smoothly, naturally.

During the stand for examination, all levels except Open and Utility, the judge directs, "Stand your dog and leave when ready," and, "Return to your dog."

When performing the First-Year, On-Leash or Novice stand, command, "Stay!" from the heel position. The rules allow "reasonable time" to position your dog physically. You may bend next to your pet to position him, but after he is in the stand position, be sure to stand up in the heel position before saying, "Stay!" and leaving. Commanding, "Stay!" while bent or kneeling next to Pooch and leaving before standing up in the heel position is bad procedure that can cost points. Stand up, command, "Stay!" then leave, going six feet away but no farther than that.

Since any dog that shows shyness or aggression is scored zero, conditioning should include strangers playing the judge. Stay next to Pooch the first few times, gradually moving away until you're at six feet. If your dog is nervous about being touched by strangers, *don't* punish him. That can worsen the problem. Slow the practice to a level your pet can handle. Start by having family members and friends your pet knows play the judge. Add strangers as your pal develops confidence.

This is a no-no. Judges want to see an exhibitor stand in the heel position when giving the stay command.

RECALL & FINISH

In First Year, On Leash and Novice, the judge directs, "Leave your dog," "Call your dog," and "Finish." In First Year, On Leash, "Leave your dog" means "Command, 'Stay!' and go to the end of your leash." In Novice, Graduate Novice and Open, go to the ring's other side or thirty feet.

Make sure your dog's recall attitude is good. The recall is triggered by command, but your dog should be seen as performing out of a sense of receiving permission to be with you. He should cover the distance quickly and arrive alert. It's true some breeds travel in a less-than-fiery manner, for which allowances should be made. Still, the animal that comes in whipped-dog fashion with head down and tail plastered has learned to respond "correctly" for all the wrong reasons. I tell you this because others, including judges, share my opinion, and a timid or fearful recall can not only cost points, it can affect a judge's overall perception of a dog's performance.

After the teams line up in catalog order and heel to one side of the ring, the judge directs, "Leave your dogs," and, after the required time, "Return to your dogs." On "Leave your dogs," command, "Stay!" and depart (to leash's end in First Year and On-Leash; to the ring's other side or thirty feet in Novice).

During stays, stand still—but naturally, not rigidly—with your hands at your sides. If you feel an itch, ignore it. A judge could decide your hand movement is a signal to your dog. Don't talk to anyone. Showing is a team effort, and you're on a stay too.

Don't stare at your dog during stays. Look toward him, but avoid a locking of eyes. Your pet may be feeling stress, and staring can heighten nervousness and cause movement.

After any stay, after the judge has said, "Return to your dog," walk counterclockwise around Pooch to arrive in the heel position. Glance at but don't stare at your dog; he may be feeling some ring stress, and a pointed look from you could lead him to move. Stand motionless until the judge says, "Exercise completed." You may then praise your companion.

Praise lightly after a stay, especially the sit-stay. The down-stay is next, and stimulating praise can excite a dog that then has to bury his fire to hold another stay. Make the upcoming stay easier by keeping Pooch calm and settled. Save any excited praise for after you've left the ring.

In First Year, On Leash and Novice, the judge directs, "Down your dogs," "Leave your dogs," and "Return to your dogs." "Down your dogs" means "Command Pooch to lie down."

FIRST YEAR, ON LEASH

First-Year and On-Leash requirements are the same. The two categories exist because a student can enter First Year only once. Youngsters who successfully complete First Year and want to enroll a second dog can do so in On Leash if the student isn't ready for a higher level. First-Year, On-Leash exercises are performed on lead.

Following is a list of exercises and the total points available for that exercise.

Heel and Figure Eight (50)

Stand for Examination (30)

Recall and Finish (30)

Sit-Stay for One Minute (45)

Down-Stay for One Minute (45)

NOVICE

These exercises are the same as those required by the American Kennel Club (AKC) for the Companion Dog (CD) title. All exercises, except heel on leash and figure eight, are off leash.

Heel On Leash and Figure Eight (40)

Stand for Examination (30)

Heel Off Leash (40)

Recall and Finish (30)

Sit-Stay for One Minute (30)

Down-Stay for Three Minutes (30)

GENERAL

Procedures are the same as in First Year and On Leash, except the down-stay is for three minutes.

GRADUATE NOVICE

For this and subsequent levels, hand your leash to a steward upon entering the ring.

Heel and Figure Eight (45)

Stand for Examination (30)

Drop on Recall (30)

Recall Over High Jump (35)

Sit-Stay for One Minute with Handler Out of Sight (30)

Down-Stay for Three Minutes with Handler Out of Sight (30)

GENERAL

Except for the recall over high jump and the drop on recall, and the fact there there's no on-leash work, Grad Novice procedures are the same as Novice's.

The judge's instructions are the same as used in the Novice recall: "Leave your dog," "Call your dog," and "Finish." After leaving your dog in a sit-stay at least eight feet from the jump, walk past the jump—don't step over it—and stand facing it from at least eight feet.

For direct retrieve, the judge's instructions are, "Leave your dog," a signal to drop the dog, a second "Call your dog" and "Finish." Sometimes before saying, "Leave your dog," a judge will direct you to drop Pooch at a given point, rather than signal you while the animal is moving.

After the judge directs, "Leave your dogs," the handlers walk to the other side of the ring, turn and face their pets. The judge then directs the group to leave the ring. After sufficient time has passed, the handlers are summoned to the ring. They line up along the side opposite their dogs. The judge then says, "Return to your dogs." Timing begins with "Leave your dogs," not when the handlers leave the ring.

OPEN

Open routines are those required by the AKC for the Companion Dog Excellent (CDX) title. The judge must approve the dumbbell used for retrieving.

Heel and Figure Eight (40)

Drop on Recall (30)

Retrieve on the Flat (20)

Retrieve Over High Jump (30)

Broad Jump (20)

Sit-Stay for Three Minutes with Handler Out of Sight (30)

Down-Stay for Five Minutes with Handler Out of Sight (30)

HEEL AND FIGURE EIGHT

These are the same as in Graduate Novice.

DROP ON RECALL

This is the same as in Graduate Novice.

Retrieving instructions are, "Throw it," "Send your dog," "Take it," and "Finish." You may command, "Stay!" before throwing the dumbbell. If it bounces significantly off-line, ask the judge for a second throw. "Take it" means "Take the dumbbell from your dog."

The judge's instructions are the same as for the retrieve on the flat. You may give only one command for the combined act of jumping and retrieving.

The judge's instructions are, "Leave your dog," "Send your dog," and "Finish." After "Stay!" and leaving Pooch at least eight feet from the nearest hurdle, go to a spot to the right and two feet from the farthest hurdle; stand facing that hurdle. As your pet jumps, turn toward where he'll land, leaving room for him to finish.

SIT-STAY AND DOWN-STAY

Except for duration, these are the same as in Graduate Novice.

UTILITY

These exercises are the same as those required by the AKC for the Utility Dog (UD) title. You must furnish three clean white gloves and two sets of five each scent-retrieve articles.

Hand-Signal Routine (40)

Scent Discrimination (30–60 per article)

Directed Retrieve (30)

Stand from Motion/Recall to Heel (30)

Send-Away and Directed Jumping (40)

Heeling instructions are the same as in preceding levels. During heeling, the judge also directs, "Stand your dog," and "Leave your dog," and then signals the handler to signal the dog to lie down, sit, recall and finish, in that order. You must remain silent during the routine.

For scent retrieve, the judge's instructions are, "Send your dog," "Take it," and "Finish." Two articles must be retrieved, a leather one, then a metal one. After scenting the article and giving it to the judge, you and your dog must face away from the articles while the scented one is placed. When told, "Send your dog," you and Pooch turn to face the articles; the animal must sit at heel before being sent to retrieve—he cannot be sent as a continuation of the turn.

For the directed retrieve, you and your dog must face away from the gloves while they are being placed. When the judge directs, "One," "Two," or "Three" (referring to the glove your dog should retrieve, reading from left to right), you turn in place, right or left at your option, and face the designated glove as your dog sits. You then signal with your left hand and verbally command your dog to retrieve the proper glove. After the dog returns, the judge directs, "Take it," and "Finish."

Upon the judge's direction, "Forward," heel your dog straight ahead. After about ten paces the judge will say, "Stand your dog," which you command verbally and/or with a signal and continue ahead without pausing—don't stop next to your pet to give the stand-stay command. After ten to twelve paces, turn and face your dog. The judge approaches the animal from the front, "goes over" it in modified conformation-ring fashion and then directs, "Call your dog to heel."

During the send-away, the judge's instructions are, "Send your dog," "Bar," or "High," and "Finish." After "Send your dog," you command, "Sit!" when your dog reaches the other side of the ring. In addition to the command to jump, you may use an arm/hand signal to indicate the proper jump.

The following pages provide judge's score sheets for each obedience level.

REFLECTION

Far better it is to dare mighty things, to win glorious triumphs even though checkered by failure, than to rank with those poor spirits who neither enjoy nor suffer much because they live in the gray twilight that knows neither victory nor defeat.

THEODORE ROOSEVELT

OBEDIENCE JUDGE'S WORKSHEET

GRADUATE NOVICE _____ CLASS _____ DOG NO. _____

A or B

DATE _____

SHOW _____ BREED _____

EXERCISE	MAJOR	SUBSTANTIAL	MINOR	Maximum Points	Points OFF	NET SCORE
HEEL AND FIGURE 8	☐ Unmanageable .... ☐ Unqualified heeling ...... ☐ Handler continually adapts pace to dog ..... ☐ Constant tugging on leash or guiding	☐ Improper heeling position .... ☐ Occasional tight leash .... ☐ Forging . ☐ Crowding handler .... ☐ Lagging . ☐ Sniffing .... ☐ Extra command to heel .... ☐ Heeling wide .. ☐ Turns .. ☐ Abouts .. ☐ No change of pace .. ☐ Fast .. ☐ Slow .. ☐ No sits .... Poor sits ☐ Lack of naturalness-smoothness .... ☐ Handler error	☐☐☐☐☐ ☐☐☐☐ ☐☐☐☐ ☐☐☐☐ ☐☐☐	**50**		
STAND FOR EXAMINATION	☐ Moves away before or during examination ...... ☐ Sits before or during examination ...... ☐ Growls or snaps .... ☐ Shows shyness or resentment	☐ Resistance to handler posing .... ☐ Extra command to stay .... ☐ Moving slightly during exam .... ☐ Moving after examination .... ☐ Sits as handler returns .... ☐ Lack of naturalness-smoothness	☐☐☐☐ ☐☐☐☐	**30**		

RECALL — Max: **30**

- Didn't come on first command or signal
- Extra command or signal to stay
- Moved from position
- Anticipated recall command
- Sat out of reach
- Leaving handler
- Handler arms not at side
- Stood or lay down
- Slow response
- No sit in front
- Extra com. to finish
- Leaving handler
- Touched handler
- Sat between feet
- Poor sit
- Poor finish
- Handler error
- Lack of naturalness-smoothness

MAX. SUB-TOTAL — 110

LONG SIT (1 Minute) — Max: **45**

- Did not remain in place
- Goes to another dog
- Stood or lay down before handler returns
- Repeated whines or barks
- Forcing into position
- Minor move before handler returns
- Minor whine or bark
- Handler error
- Stood or lay down after handler returns to heel position

LONG DOWN (1 Minute) — Max: **45**

- Did not remain in place
- Goes to another dog
- Stood or lay down before handler returns
- Repeated whines or barks
- Forcing into position
- Minor move before handler returns
- Minor whine or bark
- Handler error
- Sat or stood after handler returns to heel position

MAX. POINTS → 200

- H. Disciplining
- Shows fear
- Fouling ring
- Disqualified
- Expelled
- Excused
- Expelled
- Less Penalty for Unusual Behavior

EXPLANATION OF PENALTY

TOTAL NET SCORE →

OBEDIENCE JUDGE'S WORKSHEET

DATE _____

SHOW _____

NOVICE _____ CLASS _____

A or B

DOG NO. _____

BREED _____

EXERCISE	MAJOR	SUBSTANTIAL	MINOR	Maximum Points	Points OFF	NET SCORE
HEEL ON LEASH AND FIGURE 8	☐ Unmanageable . . . . ☐ Unqualified heeling . . . . . . ☐ Handler continually adapts pace to dog . . . . . ☐ Constant tugging on leash or guiding	☐ Improper heeling position . . . . ☐ Occasional tight leash. . . . . ☐ Forging . ☐ Crowding handler ☐ Lagging . ☐ Sniffing . . . . ☐ Extra command to heel . . . . ☐ Heeling wide . . ☐ Turns . . ☐ Abouts . . . ☐ No change of pace . . ☐ Fast . ☐ Slow . . . ☐ No sits . . . . ☐ Poor sits ☐ Lack of naturalness-smoothness . . . . ☐ Handler error	☐☐☐☐☐ ☐☐☐☐☐ ☐☐☐	**50**		
STAND FOR EXAMINATION	☐ Sits before or during examination . . . . ☐ Growls or snaps . . . . ☐ Moves away before or during examination . . . . ☐ Shows shyness or resentment	☐ Resistance to handler posing . . . . ☐ Extra command to stay . . . . ☐ Moving slightly during exam . . . . ☐ Moving after examination . . . . ☐ Sits as handler returns . . . . ☐ Lack of naturalness-smoothness . . . . ☐ Handler error	☐☐☐☐ ☐☐☐	**30**		
		☐ Improper heeling position . . . . ☐ Occasional tight leash. . . . . ☐ Forging . ☐ Crowding handler	☐☐☐			

			MAX.
LEASH	leash or guiding ☐	No sits .... Poor sits ☐ Lack of naturalness-smoothness .... ☐ Handler error ☐	
RECALL	Didn't come on first command or signal .... ☐ Extra command or signal to stay ...... ☐ Moved from position ☐ Anticipated recall command .... ☐ Sat out of reach ...... ☐ Leaving handler ...... ☐	Handler arms not at side .... Touched handler ☐ Stood or lay down Sat between feet ☐ Slow response Poor sit ☐ No sit in front Poor finish ☐ No finish ☐ Extra com. to finish ☐ Leaving handler ☐ Lack of naturalness-smoothness ☐ Handler error ☐	**35**
		MAX. SUB-TOTAL	**140**
LONG SIT **(1 Minute)**	Did not remain in place .... ☐ Goes to another dog .... ☐	Stood or lay down before handler returns ☐ Repeated whines or barks .... ☐	Forcing into position Stood or lay down after handler re- turns to heel position ...... ☐ Minor move before handler returns ☐ Minor whine or bark ☐ Handler error ☐	**30**
LONG DOWN **(3 Minute)**	Did not remain in place .... ☐ Goes to another dog .... ☐	Stood or lay down before handler returns ☐ Repeated whines or barks .... ☐	Forcing into position Sat or stood after handler returns to heel position ..... ☐ Minor move before handler returns ☐ Minor whine or bark ☐ Handler error ☐	**30**
		MAX. POINTS →	**200**

☐ H. Disciplining   ☐ Shows fear   ☐ Fouling ring   ☐ Disqualified   ☐ Expelled   ☐ Excused   Less Penalty for
 Unusual Behavior →

**EXPLANATION
 OF PENALTY**

TOTAL NET SCORE →

OBEDIENCE JUDGE'S WORKSHEET

GRADUATE NOVICE   CLASS _____

A or B

DATE _____

SHOW _____   BREED _____   DOG NO. _____

EXERCISE	MAJOR	SUBSTANTIAL	MINOR	Maximum Points	Points OFF	NET SCORE
HEEL FREE **AND** **FIGURE 8**	☐ Handler continually adapts pace to dog ☐ Leaving handler	☐ Extra commands or signals. ☐ Forging ☐ Crowding handler ☐ Sniffing ☐ Lagging ☐ Heeling wide - on turns - abouts ☐ Poor sits. ☐ Handler error	☐☐☐☐☐ ☐☐☐☐☐ ☐☐☐☐☐	**45**		
	☐ Unmanageable ☐ Unqualified heeling					
STAND **FOR** **EXAMINATION** **OFF LEAD**	☐ Moves away before or during examination ☐ Growls or snaps	☐ Extra command or signal ☐ Moving feet ☐ Moves after examination completed ☐ Sits as handler returns ☐ Handler error.	☐☐☐ ☐☐☐	**30**		
DROP **ON** **RECALL**	☐ Does not come on first command or signal ☐ Does not drop on first	☐ Stood or lay down ☐ Extra com. or sig. ☐ Before leaving ☐ Slow responses ☐ Slow return ☐ Slow drop Extra com. or sig. to stay after handler leaves. Moved from place left. Anticipate or failure to: Recall. 	☐ Touching Handler ☐ Sat between feet ☐ Poor sit. ☐ Poor finish ☐ Lack of naturalness- smoothness			

RECALL OVER HIGH JUMP Dog's Height At Withers	Refuses to jump on first command or signal ☐	Goes before command or signal ☐	Minor jump touch ☐	35
	Walks over any part ☐	Does not clear jump ☐	Poor return ☐	
		Sat out of reach ☐	No sit in front ☐	
			No finish ☐	
			Handler error ☐	
			Touching handler ☐	
			Sat between feet ☐	
			Poor sit ☐	
			Poor finish ☐	

MAX. SUB-TOTAL 140

LONG SIT (1 Minute) Handler out of sight	Did not remain in place ☐	Stood or lay down before handler returns to heel position ☐	Minor move before handler returns to heel position ☐	30
	Disturbed other dog ☐	Repeated barking or whining ☐	Handler error ☐	
			Forced into position ☐	
			Minor bark or whine ☐	
			Minor move after handler returns to heel position ☐	

LONG DOWN (3 Minute) Handler out of sight	Did not remain in place ☐	Set or stood before handler returns to heel position ☐	Minor move before handler returns to heel position ☐	30
	Disturbed other dog ☐	Repeated barking or whining ☐	Handler error ☐	
			Forced into position ☐	
			Minor bark or whine ☐	
			Minor move after handler returns to heel position ☐	

| Total score | | | **MAX. POINTS → 200** |

Less Penalty for Uncontrolled Behavior

☐ H. Disciplining ☐ Shows fear ☐ Fouling ring ☐ Disqualified ☐ Expelled ☐ Excused ☐ Other *

COMMENTS*

TOTAL NET SCORE →

OBEDIENCE JUDGE'S WORKSHEET

DATE _____

SHOW _____

NOVICE _____ CLASS _____

A or B

BREED _____ HEIGHT AT WITHERS _____

DOG NO. _____

JUMPS _____

EXERCISE	MAJOR	SUBSTANTIAL	MINOR	Maximum Points	Points OFF	NET SCORE
HEEL FREE AND FIGURE 8	☐ Handler continually adapts pace to dog ☐ Leaving handler	☐ Improper heeling position ☐ Forging ☐ Crowding handler ☐ Lagging ☐ Sniffing ☐ Extra command to heel ☐ Heeling wide ☐ Turns ☐ Abouts ☐ No change of pace ☐ Fast ☐ Slow ☐ No sits ☐ Poor sits ☐ Lack of naturalness-smoothness ☐ Handler error	☐ ☐ ☐ ☐ ☐ ☐ ☐ ☐	**40**		
DROP ON RECALL	☐ Does not come on first command or signal ☐ Does not drop on first command or signal	☐ Extra com. or sig. to stay after handler leaves ☐ Moved from place left ☐ Anticipated: ☐ Recall ☐ Drop ☐ Come in	☐ Stood or lay down ☐ Extra com. or sig. before leaving ☐ Slow response ☐ Slow return ☐ Slow drop ☐ No sit in front ☐ No finish ☐ Handler error	☐ Touching handler ☐ Sat between feet ☐ Poor sit ☐ Poor finish ☐ Lack of naturalness smoothness	**30**		
RETRIEVE ON FLAT	☐ Fails to go out on first command or signal ☐ Extra command or signal	☐ Goes before command or signal ☐ Slow ☐ Going ☐ Returning ☐ Mouthing or Playing ☐ Dropping dumbbell ☐ Poor delivery ☐ No sit in front	☐ Touching handler ☐ Sat between feet ☐ Poor sit	**25**		

OVER HIGH JUMP
Dog's Height at Withers — **35**

- ☐ Fails to jump going and returning
- ☐ Fails to retrieve
- ☐ Jumps only one direction
- ☐ Sat out of reach
- ☐ Extra command or signal
- ☐ Dropping dumbbell
- ☐ Poor delivery
- ☐ Climbing jump
- ☐ No sit in front
- ☐ No finish
- ☐ Handler error
- ☐ Touching handler
- ☐ Sat between feet
- ☐ Poor sit
- ☐ Poor finish

BROAD JUMP
2x Dog's Height at Withers — **20**

- ☐ Refuses to jump on first command or signal
- ☐ Walks over any part
- ☐ Goes before command or signal
- ☐ Does not clear jump
- ☐ Sat out of reach
- ☐ Minor jump touch
- ☐ Poor return
- ☐ No sit in front
- ☐ No finish
- ☐ Handler error
- ☐ Touched handler
- ☐ Sat between feet
- ☐ Poor sit
- ☐ Poor finish

MAX. SUB-TOTAL — 150

LONG SIT (3 Minutes)
Handler out of sight — **25**

- ☐ Did not remain in place
- ☐ Goes to another dog
- ☐ Stood or lay down before handler returns
- ☐ Repeated whines or barks
- ☐ Forced into position
- ☐ Minor move before handler returns
- ☐ Minor whine or bark
- ☐ Minor move after handler returns to heel position
- ☐ Handler error

LONG DOWN (5 Minutes)
Handler out of sight — **25**

- ☐ Did not remain in place
- ☐ Goes to another dog
- ☐ Stood or lay down before handler returns
- ☐ Repeated whines or barks
- ☐ Forced into position
- ☐ Minor move before handler returns
- ☐ Minor whine or bark
- ☐ Minor move after handler returns to heel position
- ☐ Handler error

MAX. POINTS → 200

Less Penalty for Unusual Behavior →

☐ H. Disciplining ☐ Shows fear ☐ Fouling ring ☐ Disqualified ☐ Expelled ☐ Excused

EXPLANATION OF PENALTY

TOTAL NET SCORE →

OBEDIENCE JUDGE'S WORKSHEET

Date_____ UTILITY   A   B   Armband Number:_____

Trail/Match._____   circle one   Breed of Dog:_____

EXERCISE	NON QUALIFYING -ZERO-	QUALIFYING SUBSTANTIAL	MINOR	MAXIM. POINTS	POINTS LOST	SCORE
SIGNAL EXERCISE	Handler repeatedly adapts to pace of dog Unmanageable Unqualified Heeling Failure to: ____ Stand ____ Stay ____ Drop ____ Sit ____ Come ____ . . . on the *first* command Anticipated any part Sat out of reach	Out of heel position Forge _____ Crawling Logging _____ Sniffing Fails to change pace Fast/Slow Wide heeling ____ Turns/Abouts Extra signal to heel HOLDING SIGNAL Slow response on signal to: Stand ____ Down ____ Sit ____ Come Stand ____ Down ____ Sit ____ Come No front/Finish ____ Poor Lack of naturalness/smoothness		**40**		
SCENT DISCRIMI-NATION	L M ____ Fails to go on first command ____ Fails to retrieve ____ Retrieves wrong article ____ Anticipates ____ Extra command ____ Sat out of reach	L M ____ Poor sit after turn ____ Fails to work continuously ____ Drops article on return ____ Mouthing/Playing ____ Picks up wrong article ____ Touches handler ____ Slow response ____ No front/finish poor ____ Handler error		**30** LEATHER **30** METAL		
	____ Fails to go out on command	____ Touching the dog on the send				

No front/finish —————— Poor
Lacks naturalness/smoothness

MOVING STAND — 30

Failure to:
Heel ———— Stay
Stand ———— Return
Examination
Repeated whine/bark

Forge
Lagging
Minor Movement
Handler Hesitation
Slow Response to:
Heel
Stand
Recall
No heel position poor

DIRECTED JUMPING — 40

High   Bar

Dog fails to:
Leave on command
Go substantially in the right direction
Stop on command
Take indicated jump
Climbs jump
Knocks down bar
Anticipates command
Fails to go at least 10' beyond jumps

Handler 'holds' signals
Slow response to command/signal
Dog off center (slight)
Fails to go back far enough
Anticipates ——Turn——Stop——Sit
Does not sit on command
No front/finish ——Poor
Touched handler ——Sat between feet
Lack of naturalness/smoothness

SUB TOTAL

MAXIMUM POSSIBLE POINTS 200

Handler Error ——— Fouled Ring ——— Disqualified ——— Excused ——— Less Penalty ———

TOTAL SCORE RECEIVED

DOG SHOWMANSHIP

ENTRY NUMBER ———— CLASS ———— JUDGE————

	MAXIMUM POINTS	POINTS LOST	HANDLER'S POINTS
APPEARANCE OF HANDLER Cleanliness and neatness of handler Appropriateness of apparel	**15**		
GROOMING OF DOG Brushing . . . . 5 Nails . . . . 4 Teeth . . . . 4 Ears 4	**15**		
EXHIBITOR'S HANDLING OF DOG Front Set-Up Judge's side first . . . . 2 Head High (no choking) . . . . 2 Feet typical of Breed . . . . 2 Legs typical of Breed . . . . . 2 Elbow tucked 2	**10**		
Rear Set-Up Legs typical of Breed . . . . 3 Adjust leg that is most out of line first. . . . . 4 Head not dropped while setting up hindquarters 3	**10**		
GAINING Handler in control . . . . 4 Able to follow Judge's Direction . . . . .4 Dog always visible to Judge . . . . 4 Smooth turns . . . . 4 Gait proper for Breed 4	**20**		
EXAMINATION Stand properly during Examination. . . 3 Does not growl. . . . . 4 Does not show shyness or resentment . . . . 3 (any dog biting in the ring will be dismissed)	**10**		
HANDLER'S BEHAVIOR Sportsman like behavior . . . . .10 Attentiveness to Judge. 10	**20**		
TOTAL SCORE	**100**		

See Chapter 34

32

BEFORE, DURING AND AFTER THE SHOW

Competition can be amusing and enjoyable or downright nerve-wracking, or anywhere in between. The quality of your day depends on two critical points: preparation and perspective.

Don't compete with the goal of trying to do better than any other contestants. My students and I don't try to beat anyone; we compete only against the game itself. We concentrate on doing our individual best, period. That's probably one reason why we place first so often—we aren't distracted by concerns over other competitors' achievements. Sure, we're aware of what's going on, but we focus on our own time in the ring, not on anyone else's.

When overhearing ringside comments like, "I sure hope I can beat so-and-so this time," it occurs to me the speaker is opening a door to frustration. The exhibitor will probably send nervousness down the leash, which may actually lessen his or her chances. Why? Because the person's focus is misdirected, away from the job at hand and toward a situation over which he or she has no control: the performance of competitors.

If someone scores two hundred, great! I'm happy for the person. A lot of time and effort has obviously paid off. Now, having made that acknowledgment, it's time for me to focus on my reason for entering this trial.

Another part of my competition outlook is that while it's been years since one of my dogs has bombed in the ring, I know the possibility always exists. That's part of showing. When one of mine has struck out, I found that my sleep wasn't affected and that the sun still rose in the east the following morning.

Many of us have seen a handler take a poor performance out on his or her dog. Indeed, in every endeavor some folks take part for all the wrong reasons. A competitor who needs a vent for frustration over a blown performance should start and end with a mirror. It is that person who trained the dog and who entered into competition. Pooch wasn't given a voice. If one honestly feels that landing on the animal several minutes after the fact will improve future performances, that person should learn something about dogs and seek professional help for himself.

Pets shouldn't be used to make people feel better about themselves. That puts the animals in an impossible, no-win situation. Instead of comparing or concentrating on scores or placings, compete against the performance you feel you can accomplish that day. You and your companion are after a qualifying total—anything beyond that is gravy. You should know better than anyone what you and your pal can do, and you should be equally aware of how you've done, regardless of your score. The rest is commentary.

BEFORE THE SHOW: INSTRUCTORS AND PROJECT LEADERS

JUDICIAL APPOINTMENTS

This appears in the "before" section but is of "way-before" importance—when and whom to get as judges, and whom not to get.

When? As far in advance of show time as possible.

Whom? Speak with local dog club members. Many are competition oriented and might be glad to participate. How about dog project leaders from other counties? How about former dog project students who now may have children of their own and would be willing to help? Do you teach adult classes? If so, perhaps you've a particularly apt student you could invite.

If all else fails, how about yourself? Schoolteachers generally give their own tests, you know, and some years you may not be able to find anyone as well qualified. A problem can arise from doing your own judging if you have children of your own in the program. That can open a door marked "favoritism" for those who delight in pointing fingers.

More real risks, however, are the fact that judging your own youngsters can increase pressure on them and you, and that you might be harder on your own kids.

Whom not to get is easy: anyone you yourself wouldn't want to show a dog under. Someone who is "all business," rigid, uncompromising, stern—someone lacking only top-sergeant insignia—has no business judging anyone's training efforts, least of all those of children. The ideal judge knows dogs, knows the rules, is experienced and cares about children, their feelings and their sense of self-worth. Find that in a judge and everything else will take care of itself.

SHOW SETUP

If possible, dog shows should be held wherever other events regulated by your governing body are scheduled. In the case of 4-H, often that's a fairgrounds. However, the show site should not be "that large pen where they show the sheep" ten minutes after the sheep have been there. The show site should be "clean," if you take my meaning. Showing in the "sheep pen" can be avoided by scheduling the dog show as the first event of fair week. That raises the chances of having a suitable site.

There should be sufficient room for a forty-foot-square exhibition ring, though a fifty-foot-square area is better. Also needed is adequate spectator seating and, if the show is held indoors, nonslip ring floor mats.

Appoint someone to make sure ring equipment (mats, jumps, etc.) is on hand, and someone to verify score-sheet math and to record those scores. Also, designate at least two ring stewards, to assist the judge, serve as figure-eight posts and perform all the vital tasks that make stewards such vital people.

SHOW? OR SHOWS?

In my former home county, two shows are held, one with the county fair and another a week earlier, often at the practice site. The rules provide that to earn a qualifying score, students *must* show at fair, but they *may* show at both and a qualifying score at either would entitle the student to enter state competition.* Instructors judge the first show, "to continue teaching" in the sense of offering tips while thoughts are fresh in mind.

---

*So as not to reduce fair attendance should several students qualify at the first show. We do allow students with a note from a doctor saying they were ill to miss fair competition.

Our purpose in having two official shows is to avoid grief that can occur when a student and/or his or her pet has "one of those days" in the ring. To bring the payoff of a several-months program down to a few minutes of ring time is too much pressure to put on a child. In AKC and similar forms of competition, there's always another show coming up, but the next opportunity for a dog project student is a year away, a period of time that's even longer to a child. In many regions, local leaders can override a poor county score and allow a promising student to enter state competition. But that can leave officials open to criticism from parents whose children, though they show less promise, would like the same break. The two-shows concept transfers the responsibility right back to the students, which is as it should be, but not with such force as to be overbearing.

RING? OR RINGS?

Having one ring is better than having two or three. That may be impossible in areas having large enrollments, but the idea is to allow parents whose children are at different competition levels to watch each youngster compete, which wouldn't be possible if their kids were in different rings at the same time.

SEQUENCING

The county with which I was connected runs obedience competition downward: Utility first, First Year last. This is done to have a larger audience for all students—First Year is often the largest group, and we observed in the past that after the First-Year kids showed, many parents left.

BEFORE THE SHOW: STUDENTS

DISTRACTIONS, DISTRACTIONS

The more distraction conditioning young students do with their dogs, the better they will all perform. An excellent training location is near active school playgrounds. Straight sits and the like are important, but your main focus should be keeping your dog's attention. If Pooch knows the exercises and if you can hold his attention in high-stress situations, you should experience little difficulty in competition.

SORT-OF COMPETITION

Attend as many fun matches as you can. Because they are pretend dog shows, fun matches offer ideal conditioning for the madhouse effect a show creates.

However, attend only correction matches, where ring corrections are allowed. Some matches forbid corrections, and are therefore useless and even detrimental to obedience—Pooch can learn he won't be made to obey your commands at all times.

A MINI FUN MATCH

A similar kind of conditioning is practicing under the direction of a helper acting as a judge. You get practice responding to directions, and your dog is reminded it's to listen only to you. While recently helping a friend prepare for AKC competition, I directed, "Finish!" following her pet's recall. But before she could command her dog to heel, the Sheltie did a beautiful flip finish. The animal knew the pattern and was keying on me, anticipating his owner's command.

So once in awhile delay your response to helper directives. In the case above, I told the handler to ignore my directions sometimes; to let me repeat myself several times before complying and to correct her pet if the animal responded to my cues. The idea, of course, was to teach Pooch he must listen only to his handler, not key on the pattern or on anyone else.

REMEMBER: DOGS LEARN BEHAVIOR PATTERNS

Practicing exercises in a consistent order is a trap. A dog can learn the patterns so well that he becomes bored and inattentive, or anticipates the next command. Always make your heeling turns the same way, and command using consistent pronunciation, but vary the practice sequence of the routines themselves.

OVERCOMING THE NOISE AND COMMOTION

Before showing, accustom your pet to hearing louder commands than he's used to. At a show you may have to raise your voice to be heard. If you wait until ring time to acquaint your companion with this fact, your change in volume could frighten or confuse him. TVs and radios blaring during practice can help teach Pooch to concentrate on listening only to you.

KNOW THE RULES

You should know the rules as well as any judge does. If you haven't competed before, visit with students who have. They've been there, and can be a great resource for tips and suggestions.

Novice, Open and Utility routines are based on AKC regulations. You can obtain a free copy of these rules by writing the American Kennel Club, 51 Madison Avenue, New York, NY 10010. If you are ordering more than a single copy, the price per booklet is fifty cents.

MAKE A CHECKLIST

Before going to a show, make certain you pack extra equipment (leash, collar, etc.), grooming supplies, a first-aid kit and, if you're traveling out of town, dog food and drinking water. Changing water from city to city can produce a remarkable stomach upset for your pet. A capful of "ReaLemon" in your pet's water can be a preventative, but it's still safer to bring water from home.

APPEARANCE

Yes, you're showing in obedience, not conformation. No, that doesn't mean you shouldn't be nicely attired and your dog shouldn't be reasonably groomed. You needn't go to the lengths required in breed or showmanship rings, but Pooch should be clean and brushed and his nails should be trimmed. Your appearance and that of your pet can affect attitudes: yours, your dog's and the judge's, any of which can affect your score.

DURING THE SHOW

WHEN YOU ARRIVE

Ease your dog into the show's commotion by putting its mind to rest, literally. At any show, a semiquiet spot can usually be found. Seat yourself at such a place, ignore all that's going on around you and encourage your pet to stretch out for a nap. Given time, a sound animal will lie down and very often will take advantage of the opportunity for an unscheduled snooze.

After awhile, gently wake your dog and take him from the show site for a walk. When you return, Pooch will be more at ease than when you first arrived. Why? Because once a dog has been at a place, and especially if he has slept there, he feels more at home the next time he's there, even if the occurrences are just minutes apart.

WARM-UPS

Don't practice at a show. It's against the rules and the penalties can be harsh. You're allowed to heel your pet to the exhibition area—that's practical obedience—but training at the show is forbidden. Besides, such practice is useless. If Pooch isn't ready by show time, he won't be because of a last-minute workout. If anything, he'll be tired from the cramming.

BE ON TIME

The heading "Be on Time" says it all. Understand, though, that promptness is not just a courtesy to the judge—it's a requirement. I've seen handlers breeze in with an "I'm here now" attitude, only to learn their number had already been called and they wouldn't be allowed to compete. If you have a ring conflict, which can happen when you're required to be in a conformation ring and an obedience ring at the same time, most obedience judges will try to work you in when they can. Get permission from the obedience judge beforehand, though, or you may be in for a letdown.

RING NERVES

Telling someone, "Now, don't be nervous in the ring," is like telling a child not to fear the dark—it doesn't work. "Ring nerves" is a condition like "stage fright" that lessens with time and experience.

HEELING PATTERNS

Heeling patterns account for much of a total score. Some folks suggest exhibitors study the pattern the judge is using so they know what to expect. That can be a trap. True, judges seldom change a pattern, but it can happen. The result can be a student who expected one thing but was then told something else and was momentarily confused. I prefer to hit a ring cold and listen to what the judge tells me to do.

RING CORRECTIONS

You may *not* correct your dog in the ring. That can result in disqualification. If your pet doesn't do an automatic sit during heeling, for instance, all you can do is stand there and wish he had. Of course, if your dog should start a fight, or snap at someone, yank him away right then—don't wait to be told what to do.

YOU'RE ALSO BEING GRADED

Obedience is a team effort. Your actions, as well as your dog's, are being judged. That's why score sheets include a *Deduction* section captioned

"Handler Error." In addition to preparing your dog, practice your handling technique.

DOUBLE COMMANDS

You're allowed a single command for each action by your dog. However, know there's more than one type of command.

I once saw an adult nearly have a sputtering fit after challenging a judge over his score in an AKC Novice ring. The judge told the man that he'd double-commanded repeatedly during on- and off-leash heeling. The man claimed this was not so; that he'd said, "Heel," only once whenever he moved his dog. The judge acknowledged that while it was true the man gave but one spoken command with each start of heeling, it was equally true that every time he stopped he loudly stamped his foot, cueing the dog to sit. Somewhat red-faced, the exhibitor shuffled away muttering, and I mentally tipped my hat to the judge for her integrity.

JUDGES ARE HUMAN, TOO

Like anyone else, judges can make mistakes. For example, have you ever gotten "right" and "left" backward? Even for just a few seconds? Well, a judge can too. During heeling, a judge once told me, "Left turn," as I was passing the ring gate, which was to my left. But the judge had said, "Left turn," so that's what I did: turned left and went out of the ring. The judge stopped me, called me back, apologized, said something about it being "one of those days" and we continued the heeling pattern.

I felt the judge had probably just gotten his right and left backward, but you never know—it was also possible he wanted to see what I'd do. Moral: Do what the judge says.

BETWEEN EXERCISE

As each routine ends, the judge directs the handler to move Pooch to a given spot to begin the next routine. Don't heel your pet; say something like, "C'mon, [dog's name]." Reason: If your dog heels badly the judge may notice it. True, you're between exercises and in theory no points can be deducted. Equally true is some judges may find a way to reduce your score based on what they see between exercises. Lesson: Don't do anything in the ring you don't have to do.

TO CHEAT OR NOT TO CHEAT?

Forget it. A person might get away with this or that little trick in the ring, but it's nearly impossible to cheat one's way to a ribbon. Besides, cheaters only fool themselves. Sound training is not only easier, it's more productive.

"I WAS ROBBED!"

Do judges cheat? I've not experienced it. Most obedience judges are considerate, helpful people who prefer their classes do well. Some may be tough or easy on an entire group, but exhibitors generally receive equal treatment. It's true that one judge may deduct more or fewer points for the same violation than another, but that's a problem of the system. If you and your dog successfully perform the routines in accordance with the rules, you should do well every time.

AFTER THE SHOW

POLITENESS

Regardless of how things go for you in the ring, it's simple courtesy to thank the judge and congratulate the winners. Listen up if you're offered suggestions, and appreciate the extra time.

While you're at it, look up your dog project leaders and thank them, too.

TAKE THE TIME

Find a quiet spot, away from the noise and confusion. Relax. Pet your companion. Tell the animal how proud you are of him. Show Pooch how important he is to you. Some folks say a dog can't understand the meaning of "I love you." I think they're wrong. Try it. See what you think.

ON COMPETITION

A person who puts sincere effort into training and showing shouldn't blame him- or herself if things don't go well. Best is best, and it's difficult to rehearse for all that can happen at a dog show. A nonqualifying score or last-place finish doesn't mean handler or dog is a loser; they're merely more experienced.

By the same sign, a professional leaves the ring without sharing disappointments with his or her canine teammate. Dogs can't handle human emotional loads; negative feelings teach only nervousness. When I overhear, "My dog let me down today," I feel sorry for the animal. I'm not suggesting the dog understands the words, but surely he understands the tone. (It's also tempting to remind the speaker it was he or she who trained the dog, obviously not too well.) Win, lose or draw, make sure your dog knows he's always your companion, and that he's always number one.

REFLECTION

If the horse does not enjoy his work, the rider will have no joy. If the rider is not in harmony with the nature of the animal, the animal will perform its tasks as though burdened, with no display of pleasure.

XENOPHON

CONFORMATION TRAINING AND SHOWING

GROOMING

33

Dog projects offer instruction in basic grooming of man's best friend. Further, many local projects require all dogs be properly groomed before each week's class. This is as it should be because students should perform basic pet grooming at least weekly. That's a responsibility of dog ownership. Bathing, ear cleaning, toenail clipping and brushing are essential obligations that any pet owner can and should learn. Not only do such attentions produce a cleaner animal likely to enjoy better health, the physical contact heightens bonding.

Professional grooming is rarely taught through children's dog projects since it's highly specialized work that calls for skilled, experienced hands and a considerable cash outlay for equipment. Also, precise grooming requirements—that is, the finer points—vary from breed to breed. Some will vary so much that even professional groomers have to grab a reference book from time to time to determine proper grooming for a breed they may not be familiar with.

Asking the person who bred your dog for grooming help can be a good approach. You can also visit with professional groomers for tips pertaining to your pet, but be sure those you ask know your breed. Many good grooming books and breed books with grooming chapters are available, so read everything you can find on grooming your breed.

BRUSHING

Brush Pooch weekly, more often if needed, such as when he's shedding. Be aware, though, that depending on coat type, brushing too often can make a dog's skin sore. Ask a professional groomer to recommend brushes and combs appropriate for your dog's breed and coat type.

Brush with, not against, the grain or lay of your dog's coat. Start at the neck, then do the chest and front legs. Next brush the back, sides and underbelly. Finish by doing the rear legs and tail.

If your dog's coat is slightly matted, or if the animal is shedding, apply a detangling lotion (or spray) and allow at least five minutes for the product to work before brushing. If your dog's coat is heavily matted, you may wish to have a professional groomer deal with the condition. Then avoid such problems in the future by brushing your pet regularly.

The job of brushing small-to medium-sized dogs can be made easier by placing Pooch on a sturdy table. Take care that the animal doesn't jump off and cause injury to himself.

BATHING

Thoroughly brush your pet before bathing him. Not only is there little sense in cleaning loose hair, bathing an unbrushed dog creates an unholy mess that can leave you wearing as much hair as the dog. Bathing a longhaired dog in matted condition before brushing will make grooming a terrible ordeal for you and your pet. Also, the wet hair can easily plug up a drain, especially if the dog is shedding.

If this is your pet's first bathing experience, trim and file his toenails first (see the toenail trimming section in this chapter). Some dogs become unduly excited during a first cleansing, and smoothed nails can lessen your risk of being scratched. After your dog is accustomed to this attention, you might want to work on the nails after the bath. The outer cuticle will be a little softer and so the manicure becomes easier on your pet.

Bathe your pet in a confined location, such as a bathroom, a garage (make sure there's a floor drain) or a small fenced area (ask your parents to suggest a good location). This lessens thoughts of flight or playtime, to some degree at least. Also, work on as much of a nonslip surface as possible to prevent injury to your pet as well as to you—soap and water can combine to produce very slippery conditions.

If you bathe Pooch in a bathtub, place a rubber mat on the bottom of the tub to help keep the animal from slipping. If yours is a small dog, bathing him in a sink may be easier and safer than in a tub.

Plan on getting somewhat damp yourself. That's not a defeatist attitude; it's realistic, especially during a first washing. In any event, dress accordingly. Also, if your pet should shake himself unexpectedly, dousing you in the process, don't give him the devil for being a dog. Dogs do things like that. Accept the incident as part of caring for your pet; be glad you had the foresight to wear old jeans, a T-shirt and tennis shoes, and get on with the job.

With Pooch wearing a nylon collar (for control), work backward and down from the neck area. First wet the neck, the front legs, then the withers (shoulders), back, sides and underbelly, and finally the rear legs and tail. Take care not to let water (or soap) get in your dog's eyes, ears or nose. Use warm (but *never* hot) water if possible—cold water can chill a dog. Keep the force of the water pressure low—a dog will try to get away from water applied at high pressure, understandably. One-handed petting of your dog's withers throughout the wetting, soaping and rinsing stages can deter (if not totally prevent) shaking or thoughts of flight. Gently talking to your companion during the proceedings can also help keep it settled.

Once Pooch is thoroughly soaked, apply a mild liquid soap in a gentle, massaging action. I prefer baby shampoo as it seems to be gentlest should some get in the dog's eyes. You will find many kinds of dog shampoo available; many are tearless, and some even brighten your dog's particular coat color. Follow the pattern used for wetting the animal: neck to tail, working the lather through the coat all the way to the skin. If you're bathing a large dog, rinse soaped areas as you go, to prevent the soap from being on too long. During rinsing, make sure to remove *all* traces of soap, lest it irritate the skin.

If your dog is longhaired, a cream rinse after bathing may be helpful. As with soap, follow all directions, and be sure to remove all traces of the rinse.

Do your pet's head last. Skip the use of soap; settle for gently rubbing Pooch with a warm, thoroughly soaked cloth.

The easiest way to dry a dog is to first allow him to shake a few times. Then thoroughly towel the animal. If you use a hand-held hair dryer, set the heat very low—or to no heat at all—and move it constantly at a sufficient distance so as not to risk burning your dog. If you don't use a dryer, be sure the dog is thoroughly dry before exposing it to drafts or breezes. Dogs whose coats mat easily should be brushed while drying to prevent water mats.

How often Pooch is bathed depends largely on how often he needs it. If the animal takes on a "doggy odor," of course he needs a bath. Misting Pooch with Listerine can somewhat mask the smell, but it doesn't cure the problem. Your veterinarian or groomer can tell you the best bathing schedule for your pet.

TOENAIL TRIMMING

This grooming chore makes some owners nervous, their concern being they'll nick the quick (the primary blood vessel within the nail) and cause bleeding. Nail trimming is easy to learn, however, and if performed weekly, most dogs' nails will stay at an acceptable length. If a nail should be cut too short, Kwik-Stop or a similar product (including a styptic pencil) quickly applied can halt minor bleeding, as can rubbing the nail with a wet bar of soap.

The type of nail clipper one uses is a matter of preference. Though many folks like the guillotine-type trimmers, I prefer the scissors-style variety. Some scissors-style nail cutters have a metal shield that, in theory, prevents cutting a nail too short; the metal flange supposedly keeps too much of the nail from being inserted into the cutting area. I've found this to be more of a gimmick than an effective aid, however. In many cases, especially those involving small dogs, the device actually encourages an excessive cut, allowing too much of the nail to be placed between the blades. I rely on my own judgment about the right amount to clip, and I suggest you do the same.

There is simply no way to describe the precise amount of nail to cut without risking injury to your pet. If you're unsure how much nail to remove, speak to your veterinarian or to a professional groomer. Either should be able (and willing) to show you how to tell how much nail to clip. Keep in mind, too, it's better to take off too little than too much. You can always remove more.

Though you may need the help of a family member or friend to help you trim Pooch's nails, it's preferable to do the job without assistance, if possible. Help may not always be available, and your dog should be taught that nail clipping is nothing to fear. Besides, a second person restraining your dog can actually trigger fright. Dogs often become fearful when held immobile. Also, be aware that some animals are more foot sensitive than others. They don't choose to be that way: The condition is chosen for them as a product of nature and, often, of learning. Take your time and be patient, and remember that force is seldom useful when dealing with a nervous dog. Pressure in that instance often makes a bad situation worse.

Filing a dog's clipped nails is an extra step that many owners need not take, but when showing a dog in breed or showmanship, it can be an extra plus to the judge. It says you went that extra mile in readying your dog for the ring. Metal files designed for the purpose are preferable for the task.

EAR CLEANING

Though alcohol is often used to clean ears, I prefer liquid products made for the job. Ask a groomer or vet to recommend one to you. Apply the liquid to a gauze pad and thoroughly dampen the inside of your pet's ears, wiping them dry with a second pad. As far as how deep into the ear is too deep to clean, again I suggest you confer with your vet or professional groomer.

OBESITY

When one ponders the subject of dog grooming, thoughts of soap, water and brushes generally come to mind. Grooming is a type of maintenance (as well as an expression of caring), however, and allowing a dog to become markedly overweight is a poor form of either. Not only is an obese dog hard on the eyes aesthetically, the viewer knows the animal's life span is being threatened. That's when one has to wonder just how much the owner truly cares for the animal. No dog's heart was ever meant to pump through excess layers of fat.

To give you an idea of how strongly some people feel about this point, be aware that more than one judge has told me they will "find a way" to mark down breed, showmanship or obedience exhibitors whose dogs are clearly and excessively overweight, regardless of the quality of showing and performance.

If your dog is more than marginally heavy, speak to your vet about the problem and follow his or her recommendations. More than mere ring points may be on the line—much more!

REFLECTION

The truth I do not stretch or shove
When I state the dog is full of love.
I've also proved by actual test,
A wet dog is the lovingest.

OGDEN NASH

34 BREED SHOWING AND SHOWMAN- SHIP

CONFORMATION VERSUS OBEDIENCE

Compared to conformation work, obedience judging is *objective*. The judge's score sheet lists the required exercises; the dog's performance is compared to that list on a *yes-no-sort of* basis. If Pooch sits when told to, lies down on command, heels properly and so on, he's obedient.

Sure, gray areas exist—how straight is a straight sit at heel?—but there's no mistaking a sitting dog from one that isn't, or a dog that retrieves from one that doesn't. Such acts are *objective*—they can be seen and evaluated. If a handler says, "Stay!" and Pooch runs off, the animal didn't stay. That's easy to determine.

Breed judging is trickier because it's *subjective*. Breed judges look for the dog that most closely matches the model—the ideal—he or she has in mind for the breed. However, judges can differ in their views of what constitutes a prime example of a given breed. One judge may think a dog is a good breed representative; another may look at the same animal and see weaknesses. That's why breed judging is *subjective*: It's a matter of opinion and interpretation of each breed's written Standard.

BREED SHOWING VERSUS SHOWMANSHIP

Breed showing and showmanship are alike in routine yet different in focus. Breed showing addresses the question, How good is the dog?;

showmanship is concerned with, How well is the dog shown by the handler? There's some overlap in breed showing—a very nice breed specimen that is poorly handled will not be as successful as if the animal were shown well. In showmanship, however (also referred to as breed *handling*), each dog's breed attributes are of little importance; the accent is on the student's presentation of his or her animal in the ring.

SHOWMANSHIP DIVISIONS

Showmanship is divided into Junior and Senior classes. In the local 4-H project I was connected with, Senior showmanship is for students who are fourteen years of age or older by January 1 of the current year. Junior showmanship is for anyone younger.

BREED-SHOWING DIVISIONS

Breeds are initially shown against one another: Beagles against Beagles, Dobermans against Dobermans, and so on. The winner of each breed is then shown in Group competition. Finally, all Group winners compete for top honors, usually known as *Best in Show.*

Breeds may compete directly in Group in instances where only one member of a given breed is being shown. For example, if only one Golden Retriever and one Labrador Retriever are entered, there may be little point in running one class for Goldens and another for Labs. The two animals would simply proceed to Sporting Group competition. Such instances often can occur in sparsely populated locales.

Mixed-breed animals are shown in the breed class the dog most closely matches.

The official Standards for each AKC-recognized breed with the exception of those most recently added to the list are included in *The Complete Dog Book* by the American Kennel Club, published by Howell Book House. This book is updated periodically, so be sure you own the most current edition.

BREED-RING ATTIRE

Don't overdress for the judge. You're there to show your dog, not to stage a fashion revue. Outlandish garb can distract attention from your dog to you.

Wear a color that makes a flattering background for your pet. You'll present Pooch better by wearing a color that provides a sharp

Your attire should create a contrasting background for your dog to stand out against.

The background for this dog not only doesn't contrast well, the design on the handler's shirt detracts from the dog.

contrasting backdrop against which the animal will be silhouetted as you set him up. A white dog against a white background, or a dark one against a dark background, tends to become lost visually. A white dog against a dark background, or a dark dog against a light background, stands out in eye-catching fashion.

Wear comfortable shoes that permit you to move freely while gaiting your dog. Tennis shoes are recommended, and white tennis shoes often go well with any color outfit unless you are showing a small white dog such as a Maltese or a Bichon Frise. In those cases the shoes could create optical confusion. Above all, avoid heels or sandals. Not only are they uncomfortable, they restrict movement and are noisy at indoor show sites.

Girls: Skirts, culottes or nice dress slacks are a good choice. Remember, you will be bending over your dog and gaiting it, so wear something comfortable.

Boys: Wear dress slacks or dress jeans along with a nice dress shirt that provides a contrasting background for the dog. A tie is also recommended.

LEASHES AND COLLARS

I prefer one-piece, nylon leash/adjustable-collar equipment for two reasons. First, there's one less piece of equipment to keep track of. Second, it's lightweight and—because the collar isn't metal—Pooch has an easier time distinguishing that we're doing stop-and-stand breed showing, not stop-and-sit obedience.

Whatever your preference for leash and collar, the color of the leash should match your dog. Unlike the suggestions regarding attire, the lead should not stand out. If you have a black dog, use a black lead. The idea is not to distract the judge's attention from your pet to the lead.

Snug the collar high on the neck to avoid a goose-neck appearance. Make sure hair isn't bunched up under the collar, and hold the lead in your left hand.

PRACTICE

There are four areas to concentrate upon when practicing conformation work. One is the mechanics, the nuts-and-bolts of breed-ring showing: Stacking Pooch, baiting, gaiting through the various patterns and studying ring rules and procedures until you know them as well as a judge. Second is refining your handling technique until it's smooth, coordinated and reflexive, if not second-nature. Third is capturing your dog's unwavering attention, to the point where the animal isn't just indifferent to nearby events, it's oblivious to them: It sees only you. Last, though first in importance perhaps, is training your pet to sparkle, to let out its feelings of pride in itself for all to see.

As your attitude should say "My dog's a winner!" your pet's aspect should proclaim "I'm a winner!" too. How to "teach" your dog this? Start by recognizing it already knows it. All normal beings are born with good feelings about themselves—what could be more justified in feeling good about itself than any act of creation? Then believe in the animal. Whether your pet is a splendid purebred from top bloodlines or a crossbred from the humblest origins, you know it is a one-of-a-kind thing of beauty; and you couldn't be more proud of the fact that Pooch is *your* one-of-a-kind thing of beauty. Communicate these beliefs to your pet. How? Simply tell your dog what you feel for him until your relationship is like sunlight to daytime. No, your dog will never understand the dictionary meaning of your words, but that doesn't matter; he'll understand your tone.

RING PROCEDURE

Assuming the same person judges all classes, which is often the case in many competitions, watch the class ahead of yours. Note how the class is run, what gaiting patterns (more about them in a moment) are used and so forth. Though there's no guarantee the judge will conduct your class in the same fashion, chances are he or she will. By observing the class ahead of yours, you'll be better prepared than students who don't take note of the proceedings.

There are five stages to breed presentation/showmanship:

1. Entering the ring

2. Lining up and stacking

3. Individual inspection

4. Gaiting

5. Judge's selection

ENTERING THE RING

After lining up in proper order outside the ring, a process supervised by the judge or a steward, or both, the class enters the ring when signaled by the judge. Gait your dog on your left side in a counterclockwise direction (if the judge directs a clockwise pattern, keep your dog on your right), so your dog is between you and the judge. Make sure you have adequate space relative to the dogs in front of and behind

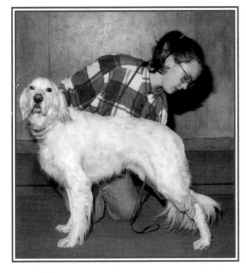

Reaching under Pooch to pose a rear leg.

you. Don't crowd the handler in front of you, and if the handler behind you is too close, ask him or her to back away.

Two important points: First, never position your dog so you are between him and the judge. A good handler never obstructs a judge's view of a dog. Second, keep an eye on the judge for cues and instructions. A judge made to feel ignored may return the favor.

LINING UP AND STACKING

After the class has gaited around the ring several times, the judge will direct the handlers to line up their dogs, often along one side of the ring. Pose yours while keeping track of what the judge is doing. It's poor form to stare constantly at the judge, but you should *always* be alert for the judge's cues. Keep your pet properly show-posed unless otherwise instructed by the judge, and move your dog forward in the line as each animal is individually inspected and then moved to the end of the line.

To pose (stack) your dog, set up the animal's front end first. The front legs should not turn out at the elbows; they should remain close to the chest. Maintain control by holding the collar, and grasp a front leg at the elbow and lift and place the foot so the leg is perpendicular to the ground and solidly under the dog. Repeat the process with the other leg. Don't place one foot ahead of or behind the other and be sure the toes point straight ahead.

Next, position the dog's rear legs. Grasp the stifle joint (rear elbow) and place each leg so the hocks are perpendicular to the ground and parallel to each other with the toes pointed straight ahead. Each rear foot should be about an inch outside the front paw location. When positioning the rear leg farthest from you, it may be better to reach under the dog than over its back. With a large dog it's not only easier to reach the leg in this manner, you are less likely to move it by bumping it with your arm.

A dog nicely posed.

And one that isn't.

And another whose feet are poorly placed.

Are you in there? Sure, we exaggerated this hair-in-the-face shot to make a point, but I've seen lesser errors make the difference between winning or not winning first place.

When placing the dog's legs, don't grasp the lower leg or the foot—that can cause the animal to move the leg once you remove your hand. Also, position the front and rear legs wide enough apart as to present a strong appearance. Placing the legs too closely together can cause a weak or even a swaybacked look.

Be aware that some breeds are posed in a slightly different stance than the one described above. The German Shepherd Dog, for instance, is stacked with a rear leg positioned somewhat under the animal's body. Verify the correct show stance for your pet by consulting a breed book or your dog's breeder. For mixed-breed animals, use the stance for the breed your dog most closely matches.

BAITING

Baiting is a breed-ring technique for capturing and holding a dog's best attention; to cause a dog to produce an expression of alert concentration. Pooch is taught to maintain his show stance and fix his total attention on the bait object, usually a food treat, and to catch the morsel when the handler tosses it to him, ignoring any food that's missed and falls to the ground.

What kind of food to use depends on your dog's preference. The rule is: Whatever your dog likes most. Cheese is a popular choice, as are liver, hot dogs and chicken, especially if they have been cooked with a little garlic.

To teach a dog to bait, first position him in the proper show stance. Then move slightly in front of the animal, keeping him in place with light pressure from the fingers of one hand on his chest as you hold the bait with the other. Briefly wave the tidbit under Pooch's nose so he can catch the scent, and quickly pull the treat several inches up and away while maintaining light fingertip pressure against his chest to keep him in place. Should the animal markedly alter his stance, quickly position him correctly and return to holding the tidbit just out of reach, moving the hand holding the goodie ever so slightly to maintain attention. After Pooch has stared at the morsel for a few seconds without appreciable movement, allow him to (gently) take it from your hand. Should the animal lunge at the food when offered to him, quickly withdraw your hand, settle Pooch and offer the food to him a second time. When giving him the snack, hold it at muzzle level and move it toward him slowly while telling him, "Easy," in a soft voice. This can teach your dog that he must take the food gently.

Teach your dog he cannot have food that falls to the ground. Hold his lead with your left hand, to keep his head up and prevent him from diving after dropped bait, and quickly recapture his attention with a

This handler is baiting her pet into the proper show stance. She keeps moving slowly backward, keeping the bait just out of the dog's reach until he achieves the desired position, when he is given the morsel.

Showing the bite.

Notice how this young handler keeps her attention on the judge at all times.

second morsel should he miss the first piece you tossed him. When tossing a treat to your dog, arc it gently toward the dog, as opposed to throwing a fastball, so to speak. The animal has to have time to see it coming in order to catch it.

If your ring attire doesn't have adequate pockets for carrying bait, wear a small bait pouch on your belt. Avoid squeaky toys and the like for baiting: They can be distractive to other dogs. Also, don't leave dropped bait in the ring. That can disrupt other handlers' attempts at control of their dogs.

INDIVIDUAL INSPECTION

The judge will direct each handler, one at a time, to present his or her dog near the front of the class, in a pose appropriate for the breed. Should the judge alter your dog's stance to one less appropriate—which some judges will do to see if you know the difference—correct the stance to the one you prefer.

An example of not listening to the judge and not being ready, and an example of the right way to do it.

Keep Pooch steady as the judge approaches and examines the animal. A helpful technique can be to place a hand at the back of the dog's head to prevent him from pulling the head away.

When showing the dog's mouth, pull the lips back to show the bite and the number of teeth. Then open the dog's mouth, keeping your hands from blocking the judge's view.

Honoring the judge.

When gaiting your dog, keep your attention on the animal, like this.

Not like this.

As the judge begins to examine your dog's front, move toward the animal's rear. Then adjust your position forward as the judge moves toward the dog's hindquarters.

GAITING PATTERNS

The purpose of gaiting a dog is to further exhibit structure and movement. The view of a dog in motion often provides clues about anatomical makeup that may not be apparent when the animal is stationary.

When told to gait your dog, listen carefully to the judge's instructions. Just because the handlers ahead of you were directed to follow a "T" pattern, for instance, doesn't guarantee the judge will have you use the same pattern.

One rule applies to each of the following six gaiting patterns: Keep your dog between you and the judge, always. Obviously, this means you must teach your pet to gait on either your right or left side, and to switch sides while in motion so as not to block the judge's view of your pet during a turn.

Just before gaiting your dog, honor the judge by turning the animal in front of him or her. During actual gaiting, align your pet and keep the animal, not you, gaiting straight, not sideways.

At the conclusion of any pattern, return to the judge for further instructions, moving your dog into a stand as you arrive. When the judge is ready for the next dog, return to the end of the line, gaiting your dog as you go—the judge may still be watching. At the end of the line, pose your dog as before.

The length of each of the following patterns is intended to correspond with the size of the ring. As a general rule, use all the ring distance available unless the judge instructs otherwise.

DOWN-AND-BACK

If there is an "old standby" in ring gaiting, it's this one. Whether you turn to the right or the left before returning to the judge—that is, when you reach the end of the *down* part of the pattern—is up to you. If you plan to turn to the right, gait your pet on your right side; vice-versa if you intend to turn to the left. The purpose, of course, is to prevent blocking the judge's view of your dog during the turn. The pattern as shown below assumes the handler has the dog to the left.

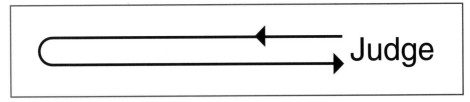

The down-and-back pattern.

"L" LEFT

The "L" pattern to the left as illustrated below assumes the handler starts with the dog to the left. At the turn designated by the letter "C," the handler should change sides so the dog is on the right, so not to obscure the judge's view.

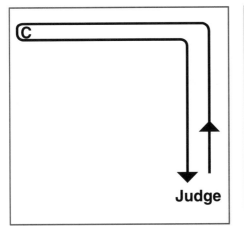

The "L" pattern to the left.

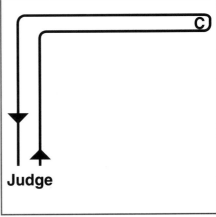

The "L" pattern to the right.

"L" RIGHT

The "L" pattern to the right, as shown below, assumes the handler starts with the dog to the right. At the turn designated by the letter "C," the handler should change sides, putting the dog on the left.

TRIANGLE RIGHT

The triangle right, shown below, allows the handler to keep the dog to the right throughout the pattern without blocking the judge's view.

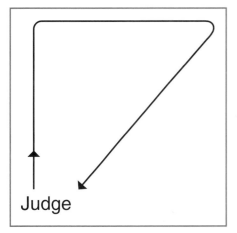

Triangle right.

REVERSE TRIANGLE

The reverse triangle (or triangle left), shown below, allows the handler to keep the dog to the left throughout the pattern without blocking the judge's view.

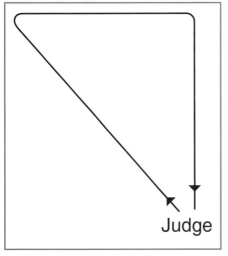

Reverse triangle.

"T" PATTERN

The "T" pattern as illustrated below assumes the handler starts with the dog to the right, changes to the left at the point marked "C1" and changes back to the right at "C2."

One constant rule in all gaiting patterns bears repeating: *Never block the judge's view of your dog!*

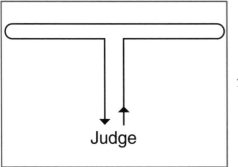

The "T" pattern.

JUDGE'S SELECTION

After the last dog has returned to the end of the line, the judge may direct handlers to move their animals to different locations within the group. Some judges will announce their placings at this point, but most will direct the group to gait their dogs around the ring a final time. In any case, decision time is at hand.

If there's ever a time to keep an eye on the judge, it's now. Soon the judge will signal his or her placings, a gesture the winning handler should immediately acknowledge.

SCORING

The end of chapter 31 depicts a judge's score sheet for breed showing and showmanship. We use this sheet locally not to aid the judge—he or she knows how to score dogs and students—but the completed sheets are given to the students to help them understand the reasons for a judge's placings.

ANATOMY LESSON

As part of conformation showing, the judge may ask you to identify various parts of your dog. Study the following drawing closely.

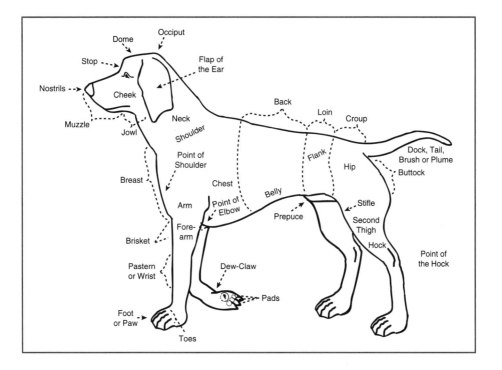

ATTITUDE: YOURS

Whether competing in breed showing or showmanship, handler attitude can play a large part in a judge's decision. You must radiate an aura of, "My! Isn't this magnificent dog of mine as close to perfect as you're likely ever to see!" Your job is not just to go through the motions of presenting a dog. Yes, correct mechanics—grooming, gaiting, stacking—are necessary to win in breed or showmanship competition. But more than that, your job is to try to "sell" the judge the idea that while there are undoubtedly other good dogs present, yours is far and away the best. How to do that? As suggested earlier, if you believe in your dog, and recognize there is no other like him in the whole world, then all you need do is let those feelings show.

PREFERENCES AND CAPABILITIES

Some students enjoy breed showing and showmanship more than they do obedience competition, and vice versa. Some breed-ring folks feel that trying to train their dogs for the dual purpose of conformation and obedience showing can cause problems in both rings. This is a valid concern. More than once I've seen dual-purpose dogs stand in place rather than automatically sit in an obedience ring during heeling, or sit in a conformation ring when the handler stopped moving.

One solution to the problem is simply to abandon one form of showing in favor of the preferred activity. Besides, if a person has no interest in obedience but enjoys conformation work, then the time spent in obedience training may be largely wasted. In the same vein, it's true that dual-purpose showing is not "right" for every dog. Though they are few, some dogs can't handle being an obedience competitor one minute, a show dog the next. Also, some animals, like some people, prefer one type of work over the other. Instead of trying to change that attitude, respect it, and appreciate the gifts your pet does have.

But what to do when a student enjoys both forms of competition and has a dog that can do well at both? How to overcome ring confusion that can arise?

First, recognize that the routines are markedly different. In obedience competition, handler and dog usually enter the ring alone, until group exercises. The handler stops a few steps after entering the ring, as opposed to gaiting Pooch around the ring, and commands, "Sit!" if need be.

Second, differences in equipment (a chain choker and leather leash in obedience, a lightweight show lead and nylon collar in conformation) can cue a dog as to the work expected. The animal learns that when his partner talks to and touches him repeatedly in a ring, it's conformation time; that silence broken only by one-word commands and intermittent praise signifies obedience. No, the dog may not "think" these things consciously, but he's aware of the differences in terms of behaviors expected of him.

Keep obedience and conformation training separate; never mix the two. Don't do obedience for a few minutes, then conformation for a few more, then obedience, and so on. Also, be sure to always use the proper equipment for the work at hand.

Now consider a concern among conformation fans: Obedience training can knock down a dog's attitude, causing it to radiate a less-than-winning aura in breed and showmanship competition. This is a legitimate concern, but it portrays a truth of a kind. The notion that obedience training in and of itself harms a dog's attitude is false; if anything, obedience training enhances canine spirit. Attitude problems that can arise from obedience training do so from *improper* obedience-training methods. These are often characterized by heavy-handed, perfectionist and unappreciative treatment by people driven to do better than others to the degree they've forgotten what's at the other end of the leash. Such mismanagement can knock down a dog's attitude toward any endeavor, not just toward breed work. Caring and compassionate obedience training, however, increases bonding, and heightened bonding can easily lead to spectacular, day-making, breed-ring performances.

PARADOX

"Which is harder: obedience or conformation?"

Based on the space each occupies in this book, readers might conclude obedience is harder. But like the notion that children can't train dogs as well as adults can, that's a myth. It's a "What you see is not what you get" illusion, as the difference is mechanical. Obedience, from First Year through Utility, covers twenty-six mechanical elements; conformation covers two.

"So, don't those numbers say obedience is harder?"

"Nope. It's just more varied."

Understand, there's work involved in both forms of training. Lots of it. All trainers have praise to fall back on, but obedience people also have force as an ally. They can "make" a dog do a given thing. But no dog can be forced to radiate a winning attitude, in a ring or anywhere else. When it comes right down to it, a breed trainer's best resource is the ability to *communicate* "Okay, baby—turn it on!" to his or her pet. That's an art that can take years to develop.

"So conformation work is actually harder?"

Until you master it. Then it becomes easier because it is ultimately more natural. It's communication at a feeling level, where dogs talk, and it's the purest form of exchange there is.

REFLECTION

I cannot give you the formula for success, but I can give you the formula for failure—which is: Try to please everybody.

HERBERT BAYARD SWOPE

ADDITIONAL CHALLENGES

35 BRACE OBEDIENCE

In brace handling, a student works two dogs at the same time. Ideally both dogs are of the same breed, size and color, but 4-H and similar organizations seldom have such requirements. The exercises are the same as those in Novice competition.

Heel on Leash and Figure Eight* (40)

Stand for Examination (30)

Heel Off Leash (40)

Recall and Finish (30)

Sit-Stay for One Minute (30)

Down-Stay for Three Minutes (30)

All exercises, except heel on leash and figure eight, are performed off leash.

The dog's collars are linked together by a properly sized coupler— a length of leather or chain material with an "O" ring in its center (to which the leash is attached) and having snaps on both ends for attaching to collars.

TRAINING

Work only with dogs that are individually proficient at Novice obedience. Two dogs can be taught Novice work while also being trained to perform in tandem, but the task is much easier if the animals already know the individual exercises.

An easy way to accustom dogs to working together is to start with the stays: sit, down and stand, in that order. For the sit-stay the dogs need do only that: sit and stay; no coordinated movement is required. For the

*Volunteers acting as posts for the figure eight should stand farther apart than the customary eight feet to allow more room for a handler and two dogs.

A two-dog coupler.

down-stay the animals must learn to lie down in unison; for the stand-stay they must be taught to move into the standing position together. This sit-down-stand-stay sequence of teaching accustoms the dogs to work together and to progressively make more movements together.

Once your pets are doing well with the stays, add on-leash heeling. Include the figure eight only after both animals are comfortable at heeling together on leash. Then progress to off-lead heeling. Once your pets are adept at this, add the recall and finish, in that order.

Keep in mind that even though your dogs know the Novice exercises, they've learned to perform them individually. They may need much time—perhaps more than you might suspect—to become proficient at working together. Practice patience born of the insight that good dogs progress as quickly as they're able.

Here are two final tips. When first linking your dogs' collars together, train using two leashes, attaching a lead to each animal's collar so a correction for one isn't a correction for both. Second, during heeling, place the quicker-working dog to the outside, since that animal will have to take more steps during heeling turns.

REFLECTION

Men are born to succeed, not to fail.

Henry David Thoreau

TRACKING

OVERVIEW

During tracking competition a dog uses its scenting ability to follow a stranger's path and locate an object the person has dropped, usually a dark glove or billfold.

But know this: Tracking isn't "right" for every dog. Sure, all breeds are born with tracking ability, but some are clearly more gifted than others. Bloodhounds top the list, sighthounds end it. Does that make one breed better than another? Better as dogs, no; better as trackers, yes. My favorite all-around breeds are Doberman Pinschers and German Shepherd Dogs, but were I a hunter, neither would be my first choice as a field companion. Every breed has its strong and weak points. Is your dog a potential track-master? An easy way to find out is to run it through the first lesson, presented below, and see how it does.

TEACHING

Introduce tracking by teaching your dog to find you. Given healthy bonding, your pet is drawn to you more than to anyone or anything on this earth. Because his motivation to find you is so high, using you as a tracking target is an excellent way to start.

You'll need the help of someone the dog knows and likes because the helper will handle Pooch during the first few tracks. You'll also need access to a large, short- to medium-cropped grassy area, preferably a remote one that doesn't experience a lot of foot traffic and is therefore relatively devoid of other human scent. The best teaching times are just after sunrise, at dusk and shortly after a light rain, in that order. That's when scent most powerfully rises from the ground. During training the wind should be still, preferably dead calm, so as not to blow scent around and create a confusing track. Bring your pet on leash to the tracking area but don't formally command him to heel. Corrections are totally out of place when teaching tracking, and were Pooch to heel poorly, you'd have to correct him or accept poor work.

Eliminate having to contend with the problem by not commanding your pet to heel in the first place.

Put a leather or nylon collar (or a nonrestrictive harness) on your dog, attach a ten-foot leash and hand it to your helper. Slide your feet back and forth over a twelve-inch-square area to create what's called a "scent pad." Then start backing away in a straight line from your dog, taking small steps and dragging your feet to lay a heavy track. Wave good-bye to your pet as you leave, saying things like, "Good-bye, [dog's name]," and "See you, [dog's name]." At the same time your helper should *whisper* (to communicate without distracting) things like, "Where's [your name] going?" You and your assistant talking to the dog like this will focus his attention on your departure and create moderate internal canine tension, which we'll soon show him how to release by finding you.

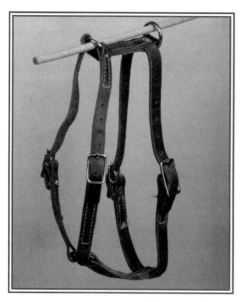

A nonrestrictive tracking harness.

After you've moved twenty feet away, turn your back to your pet and continue walking another twenty or so. Then duck behind a bush, a tree or similar natural barrier. Ten seconds later your helper should point to the scent pad and encourage, "Find!" while gesturing toward the direction you took. Your assistant may say, "Find!" as often as seems helpful—this isn't one-command obedience we're working on—but once the dog is tracking, your helper should keep silent. Telling a dog to do something it's currently doing can distract the animal. Also, your friend should stay five or six feet behind your pet once the animal puts his nose to work, again the idea being not to distract. When your dog reaches you, love up that critter while repeating, "Good find!"

IF THE DOG DOESN'T TRY TO TRACK

The dog doesn't try to track. Now what? First, your helper should have Pooch lie down on the scent pad (to focus the animal's attention on the ground), and give further encouragement to "Find!" Linking your name with "Find!" (as in "Find [your name]!") can also be helpful.

Another method is guiding the dog to you, with your assistant repeating, "Find!" along the way, and both of you excitedly praising, "Good find!" when your pet gets to you. Sure, the dog didn't track, but praising an animal as though he did a given thing can sometimes get the message across. See if it did by trying a second track.

Dropping small food bits like hot dog chunks every other step while laying a track can draw Pooch's attention to the ground. Over several weeks, drop the morsels with decreasing frequency relative to your steps.

Lay a track without your dog present. Then your helper should bring Pooch to the scent pad, point to it and encourage, "Find!" The dog may realize you're "out there," and that tracking is the only way to be with you.

Last, with your helper holding the lead, you show Pooch a food treat and start laying a track. After twenty feet, put the treat on the ground, after first waving it at your pet so he will see you put it down. Then return along the track, take the lead, point your treat-scented hand at the scent pad and say, "Find!"

That last technique is as close to "forced tracking" as I'll take you. Harsh force methods exist, but if your pet hasn't gotten the idea by now, or if he simply isn't interested, consider dropping the idea of tracking. It likely isn't "right" for him. Don't radiate any disapproval, though—your pet doesn't need that. He's done the best he's able, but just as football or chess or mountain climbing may not be right for you, tracking may not be right for your pet.

ON THE OTHER HAND

If your dog does well on the first track, lay a second track at least thirty feet away from the first one (laying tracks too close together can cause a dog, especially an inexperienced one, to be confused by the nearby, overlapping scent areas). Have Pooch find you again, then end the day's session.

The next tracking session should be a repeat of the first: your dog finding you twice. On the third day, have your dog find your helper, or a family member, twice. Each new track should be at least thirty feet from those laid the day before—many dogs can detect a day-old track and we don't want to confuse your pal.

On the fourth day, go back to laying the track yourself but this time without your dog present. Have your helper watch where you walk, so he or she knows where to start Pooch after bringing him to the training area once you're hidden. One successful track is enough for today. The next three sessions are repeats of this one, except your helper is the tracking target.

TURNS AND TOYS

Four days later add a new twist by having your helper make one right-angle (ninety-degree) right or left turn after his or her first ten to twenty steps. Your assistant should push a brightly painted wooden stake into the ground at the turn so you can be sure of the turn's exact location. You may have to guide Pooch somewhat when he reaches the turn. He's used to straight-line tracks, so you may even need to stop the animal and say, "Find!" while pointing at the ground toward the direction your helper went, to give your pet the idea.

Once your dog is doing well at finding a turn, have your assistant carry your dog's favorite play toy (which, for illustration, we'll consider a tennis ball). As your tracking whiz finds your helper, the person should throw the ball for your pet. When the animal returns with it, you should take the toy and throw it for it a few more times.

After a few days of find-the-helper, play-with-the-toy, make one subtle adjustment: Have your assistant place the ball on the track about twenty feet after the turn. That's where tracks will end from now on: where the ball is, not where the person is. After placing the ball on the track, your assistant should walk several more feet in the direction he or she was going, and should then leave the tracking site. Otherwise your dog might see or scent the individual and that could confuse him; the dog might think he should ignore the ball and seek the person. When Pooch finds the toy, excitedly say, "Good find!" and quickly throw the ball for him to chase. Your enthusiastic praise and playing with your dog with his toy now becomes your pet's tracking reward.

OVER THE NEXT FEW WEEKS AND MONTHS

Gradually make the tracks longer, until they approximate 250 paces.

Add a second turn, about fifty paces after the first one; the ball should be placed on the track several yards beyond this second turn.

Use a leash that allows you to be twenty feet behind your dog.

Gradually increase the time between when the track is laid and when Pooch is told, "Find!" until the animal is working tracks two hours old.

The keys to successfully making these adjustments are the words *gradual* and *sequential.* Don't jump from a fifty-foot track on Wednesday to a one-hundred-yard track on Thursday. Add the second turn only after your dog is doing well with one turn and longer tracks. Once he's adept at two turns, start moving yourself back farther along the lead. Slowly increase time only after your pet is used to long, two-turn tracks with you twenty feet behind him. Then only two final adjustments remain to be made: using a formal tracking article instead of a toy, and your dog signaling you of his find.

TRACKING ARTICLE

My preferred tracking article is a glove. This is because the rules usually specify a dark glove or wallet, and it's difficult to insert a tennis ball into a billfold. What do I mean by that? Just this: When I start using a glove, it's one I've stuck a tennis ball into. Pooch finds the glove, I withdraw the ball and throw it for him—that's his reward. Because he's greatly drawn to the toy, a glove (or wallet) wouldn't hold much interest for him; but once he sees that the glove contains his toy, he'll seek a glove with interest. Of course, during the tracking trial the glove won't contain the toy, but that will be the one and only time the ball won't be part of the glove, and the dog won't know not to expect the toy to be there that single time. That day I'll play with him *after* leaving the tracking area.

SIGNALING

Competition rules for 4-H and similar organizations generally follow those of the AKC. Tracking Dog (TD) regulations in the AKC format require a dog to stand in place and look at the tracking article once he's found it, or to pick it up. You may teach either style, but teaching a dog to pick up the object is often easier. This is because a dog wants to pick up his toy when finding it, and this tendency continues as the animal discovers that the glove contains his toy. During a competition track, Pooch may be a trifle disappointed to learn he can't feel his toy in the glove, but as suggested earlier, throwing the ball for him soon afterward will be ample reward.

REFLECTION

In the beginning God created man,
but seeing him so feeble, He gave
him the dog.

TOUSSENEL

CHAPTER 37

PROJECT PROBLEMS AND SOLUTIONS

This chapter is primarily intended for instructors and project leaders.

Problem: A student brings to class a dog he or she can control (restrain on a leash) but whose middle name is aggression. This is a bad-tempered animal that snaps at anything and everything in sight.

Solution: The dog must leave; he cannot stay. As stated earlier, student safety (not to mention your own) is a primary concern. It is probable that the animal's hostile tendencies are genetically based, which no training can assuredly override.

Problem: A student arrives with a sick dog.

Solution: Send Pooch home. The student may stay; the animal cannot.

Problem: A parent, for whatever reason, wishes to work with his or her child during all classes.

Solution: The individual is probably just trying to help, which should be appreciated. Take the person aside, though, and ask him or her to sit with the other adults. Point out that were all the parents to descend upon the training area, there'd be no room for the students and their dogs; that like any school situation, parents don't accompany children into the classroom. If need be, enlist the help of other parents; ask them to have a word with the person. Should the individual remain adamant, offer a final choice: Join the other parents or leave the training area.

Problem: A handicapped student wishes to enter the program and though he or she is capable of doing the work, it's apparent that much extra time and effort on your part will be needed.

Solution: That's one of the reasons you're there. Plan on arriving early and/or leaving late. This is a chance to see if your dedication matches that of such a youngster.

Problem: A student wishes to train a dog that is crippled but that seems able to do the work comfortably despite the handicap.

Solution: If the youngster believes in the dog and in him- or herself sufficiently to take on the challenges, encourage the request. However, make the student aware that depending on local rules, the dog may be barred from competition.

Problem: A stranger offers to help with the program.

Solution: Don't lose a potentially good helper, but get to know the person before allowing involvement with the kids. There is no shortage of perverts in this world, and they may see class gatherings as a treasure trove. You can never be too careful!

Problem: You suspect a student is a child-abuse victim.

Solution: Don't think you won't run into this one. Contact the proper authorities, pass along your information and let them earn their pay. Also, apprise your organizational official of your observations and of the steps you're taking.

Problem: Parents cite religious objections in refusing to have their dog vaccinated against rabies, distemper, and so on.

Solution: Your student count just decreased by one. Regardless of a person's convictions about vaccinations, you cannot risk having an unvaccinated animal on the premises.

Problem: Class is over but a parent hasn't arrived to collect his or her youngster. You have an important meeting across town in a few minutes. Another parent has offered to wait with the child until Mom or Dad arrives.

Buddies. Cel Hope, an instructor with our local program, and her German Shepherd Dog, Wonder.

Solution: Stay put. That child's welfare is more important than any reason you might have for leaving. Doubtless nothing would go wrong, given an adult has volunteered to wait with the youngster, but this way you *know* nothing unforeseen can happen.

Problem: A student is continually too tough with his or her dog and resists your "lighten up" counsel, perhaps even telling you that so-and-so's book says such "technique" is okay.

Solution: Tell the student to pitch so-and-so's book (there is some real garbage in print) and show him or her the photograph on this page. Ask, "Do you *see* what's in this picture?" Comment, "If you can get this going with your dog, you won't need such force." If the child still resists, have another instructor intervene. Visit with the student's parents. Should the youngster maintain a deaf ear, state, "My way or the highway," and mean it. To accept canine abuse is to promote it.

Problem: There's no place to store equipment (jumps, floor mats, etc.) at the practice site.

Solution: Enlist the aid of a willing parent with a large vehicle, a strong back and an available storage area.

Problem: It's the day of the show and a student tells you he or she left the leash (collar, brush, etc.) at home.

Solution: Mistakes happen, which is why you should bring extra equipment to the show. To practice sessions, no—that can teach a student to have a nonserious attitude—but to the "big show," yes.

REFLECTION

Follow your desire as long as you live; do not lessen the time of following desire, for the wasting of time is an abomination to the spirit.

PTAHHOTPE

POSTSCRIPT

This book opens by examining a myth. It closes here with a slice of reality. Consider the following account.

A person has a devoted, well-mannered dog. He and Pooch attend a few classes and someone comments the animal might do well in competition. The owner decides to try his hand, but after a few shows in which the dog doesn't do well, he recognizes his pet doesn't have what it takes. That's where the story should end, with the person seeing that though he may not have a High in Trial or Best in Show candidate, he's blessed with the companionship of a loyal, loving friend.

But sometimes a cheerless truth is the owner comes to look down on the dog, seeing what isn't instead of what is. Forgotten is the joyful greeting at homecoming, the comforting presence during unhappy times, the constant friendship offered with no strings, no thought of gain. Ring honors take on a distorted importance they were never meant to have, ultimately becoming of greater worth to the gung-ho competitor than his dog's unconditional love. Bonding weakens as the gulf widens, affection dries up and a part of the dog goes to sleep, never to waken again. More is lost than any ribbon or trophy could ever replace.

Scores and awards are fleeting and temporary, but a dog's love is forever. Accept it, cherish it and count your blessings. In all situations a sound dog does its best. It may not always succeed in pleasing, but it won't be for lack of trying. In the end, trying is all anyone, dog or human, can do.

ABOUT THE AUTHOR

Joel McMains has been training dogs professionally since 1976. In addition to offering contract obedience and protection training services, he holds public obedience classes and training seminars, and was the coordinator of Sheridan (Wyoming) County's 4-H Dog Program from 1982 to 1994. Joel is retired as the chief K-9 trainer for the Sheridan County Sheriff's Department and for the city of Sheridan Police Department. He has testified in court proceedings as an expert witness, and has taught a course in K-9 selection, management, training and deployment for the Police-Science Division of Sheridan College. Joel is a member of the Dog Writers' Association of America.

INDEX